Buzz about Bodacious! Career

"Intelligent and useful suggestions to help women find their way in today's business world"

> – Barbara Sher, author of bestseller
> *Wishcraft: How to Get What You Really Want*

"AOL insider Foley experienced vast changes in her life as she moved from a customer service job at a computer company to heading the exploding AOL company. *Bodacious! Career* is both an autobiography of her experiences and what it means to be a businesswoman in today's corporations."

> – *Midwest Book Review*

"*Bodacious! Career* is a true wake-up call for any woman who has put herself second, especially in the work world."

> – Bonnie Ross-Parker, author of *Walk in My Boots~*
> *The Joy of Connecting*

"Foley gives women readers practical advice that can both aid their advancement through corporate ranks and assist in their personal maturation."

> – Kay Hammer, author of *Workplace Warrior: Insights and*
> *Advice for Winning on the Corporate Battlefield*

"*Bodacious! Career* is by far one of the best books I have read to date. Mary inspires, empowers, and flat out tells it like it is!"

> – Tara Patterson, Founder of JustForMom.com

"I am recommending it to every female client I am working with. Not only are the angels in heaven high-fiving each other, more and more women are doing this as well, thanks to you!"

> – Chris Wahl, Coaching & Organization Development
> Consulting

"I got so jazzed while reading in your book about the importance of networking that I had to stop right there and start focusing on reaching out and connecting."

> – Carla Blazek, Creator, zenamoon.com

"I finished the book the day before I had to fire someone and I truly believe your book prepared me for the meeting. You are so right when you say that girls are brought up to be nice and we have a hard time being firm and confrontational."

— Kristina Bouweiri, CEO, Reston Limousine Service, Inc.

"I found your book very inspiring — so much so that I am going to do what I have wanted to do for years — teach aerobics/personal training in my home!"

— Wendy, Leesburg, VA

"I just read Mary's book and thought it was fabulous! I'm actually going to use the ways in the book to talk with my division manager."

— Anna, Arlington, VA

"Your book has generated a can do attitude that is out of this world! I read it in three days and it's awesome!"

— Levina, Ashburn, VA

"Sharing your insights in your book continues to inspire many of us women young and old to define and to pursue our own life's happiness. You have re-vitalized the boldness within my own spirit."

— Susan, Silver Spring, MD

"I just purchased your book and can't wait to read it. Just reading the table of contents, your bio and seeing your website I am already inspired."

— Shauna, Vancouver, BC

"I am in love with your book and want to share it with several of my friends!"

— Jessica, Nashville, TN

"Thank you for inspiring so many women to live their lives with a free spirit and bodacious will to conquer life in such a way that it lifts our spirits and ambitions to a higher level."

— Kim, Washington, D.C.

bodac!ous
career

**Outrageous
Success
for Working
Women**

Go Bodacious!

Mary Foley

Mary Foley

Bodacious! Career: Outrageous Success for Working Women
By Mary Foley

Copyright © 2004 Mary Foley

Published by
Bodacious! Books
11951 Freedom Drive, Suite 1300, Reston, VA 20190

In cooperation with
Fidlar Doubleday
6255 Technology Avenue, Kalamazoo, MI 49001

Design and layout
Scout Design
Richmond, VA

ISBN: 0-9745653-0-X

Printed in the United States of America

For more information, go to **www.bodaciouscareer.com**

For my parents, Charles and Donna Foley,
who taught me I could be anything I wanted.

Contents

3   *Take a Stand*

4   *Thrive on Shift and Change*

About the Author

Experiencing Mary is experiencing bodaciousness. At age 33, Mary Foley retired from America Online, where she started 10 years earlier as an $8 an hour customer service rep. During those years she learned that being bold, audacious, courageous – bodacious – was the only way to thrive as a woman in business in today's world. In her book *Bodacious! Career: Outrageous Success for Working Women*, Mary shares her lessons learned and strategies for career success. As author, speaker, and seminar leader, Mary empowers women to "look within, think strategically, act bodaciously, and love every minute of it!"

Mary has appeared on over 2 dozen major TV affiliates; over 100 radio stations; and in numerous newspapers and magazines including *Kiplinger's Personal Finance*, *The Boston Globe*, *The Times of London* and the *Denver Business Journal* among others. Mary also helps guide the growth of HumanR (www.humanr.com), a human resources software and consulting company, for which she is a board member and investor. She holds a bachelor's in industrial engineering from Virginia Tech and a masters in organization development from Pepperdine University. She lives in Reston, Virginia.

Preface

It's hard to do anything for 10 years and not learn something along the way. But when you're a young adult starting a career in a New Economy company long before the term was even invented, you learn, and learn lots. That's what happened to me a little over a decade ago when I joined Quantum Computer Services which became America Online, now AOL Time Warner.

Even in the midst of my ride with what's currently the world's largest media company, I knew what I was experiencing was special and unique. In fact, I considered myself corrupted and still do. I've tasted a certain sweetness – the combination of excitement, fulfillment, and frustration that comes with being part of something that ushered the Internet into the dominant digital technology of our age. In a very real sense, we changed the world, and in a very real sense I was changed as well. The lens through which I now view and experience life has been altered – corrupted – forever.

Don't get me wrong, I'm glad I'm corrupted, or should I say I feel fortunate to have been immersed in the New Economy way of doing things so early on while I was young and impressionable. Seared into my brain like indelible ink and imprinted into every cell of my body is the knowledge that a fulfilling, fun, and rewarding career is possible, that change is not only good, it's necessary for individual and corporate vitality, and that speed can thrill, kill, and push us to deliberately decide what's important to us and why. I've tasted "the good fruit" and don't want to settle for anything less!

During my AOL years, I also learned an invaluable lesson as a woman who wanted to grow in her career; being a "good girl" wasn't good enough. Good girls are nice, competent, and cooperative, but it takes more than that to be effective and create success. It takes gustiness, a willingness to take risk, and a positive attitude. It takes a deep sense of self-worth and belief in one's abilities. In short, it takes being bodacious! So significant was this discovery that I wanted to share my personal journey and lessons learned to help other working women do what's more than possible: build a Bodacious Career.

In this book, you'll learn the bodacious way for your own gain. You'll see how you can staff your career with people and relationships that help you while minimizing the rest. I'll share with you how to take a stand with others when needed and to exhibit your personal power in a positive way. I'll give you strategies to thrive on the reality of constant change. You'll see how office politics can be used for the good of your career and for others, and I'll show you how to create your own big, bodacious personal plan to create the career you want. In addition, I've included a dozen practical, ready-to-use sidebars on such topics as how to interview in the New Economy, how to tell if someone is playing power games with you, and how a little testosterone can go a long way to helping you firmly establish your newfound bodaciousness.

I'm certain you will benefit from my years at AOL. Read on and consider these lessons and strategies for yourself. Test them out, add your own style, and make them your own. Your Bodacious Career is waiting. So, go for it!

10 Bodacious Ways for a Bodacious Career

1 **Don't take it personally**

2 **Create deliberate relationships**

3 **Take the work out of networking**

4 **Actively market your value**

5 **Know how you want to be treated**

6 **Take a stand**

7 **Thrive on shift and change**

8 **Know your worth**

9 **Embrace office politics**

10 **Think strategically, act bodaciously**

Acknowledgements

It took a lot of people over a long time to affect my life in a myriad of ways to make this book possible. So, I could say thanks to everyone I've known. However, I need to single out some who had notable impact.

Thanks to all the AOLers past and present who made my work experience so rich, purposeful and fun. In particular thanks to Steve Case, Jean Case, Keith Jenkins, Mike Connors, Brian Burnett, Wendy Garcia, Norm Wilhelm, Robin Sparks, Kathy Riley, Bill Fitzgerald, and Mark Stavish. Special thanks to the very bodacious and wise Tiane Mitchell-Gordon who introduced me to SARK, the author of *The Bodacious Book of Succulence*, the book that set off my own bodacious spark.

Thanks to my family and friends whose support and encouragement sustained me more than I can describe or repay. Thanks to Mom and Dad for always loving me, period. To my siblings Leslie, Amy, and Charley, thanks for being proud of my success. I'm so proud of yours! To Ruth Hill, Suzanne Martinez, Elizabeth Faulkner, Jana Bridgman, and Michele and Diana Schick, thanks for your love and support of my high times and low. Thanks to friends who broadened my professional world and believed in my abilities: Mary Saily, Burgess Levin, Kevin Karaffa, Jim Atwood, Ray Snyder, Ken Blanchard, Laura Georgantos, Patricia Cooper, Deborah Young-Kroeger, Cindy Morgan, Chris Worley, David Hitchin, Tony Petrella, and Peter Block. Special thanks to Marta Brooks who first encouraged me years ago to capture my AOL experiences as *Wee Wee with the Big Dogs*. And, finally, special thanks to Hank, the most bodacious man I know and love, for believing in me.

Thanks to Angeline Robertson and Charley Foley of Scout Design (www.seescoutdesign.com) whose graphic design and photography excellence continues to make me look good. Thanks to Barbara Keddy (www.begreatmarketing.com) with whom I share the early days of Quantum Computer Services and is now helping me be great with her smart, Now Economy marketing.

And, thanks to the divine Creator, big kahuna, universal force, loving Lord, whom I call God. I don't know how it all works, but I do know the love, goodness, healing, and empowerment I've experienced comes from you.

Like Nothing You've Ever Seen Before

"Life's short, learn fast."

I was wearing those words of wisdom on my T-shirt the day I went to work without my pants. Yes, my pants. I showed up that day like I always did, prepared to work out in America Online's well-equipped fitness center before the work day began, wearing my workout clothes and carrying my office clothes in my gym bag to change into after my shower – after my shower. That was when I made the discovery: no pants. I had a meeting in forty-five minutes with another two in quick succession. I had no time to go home and change, especially in the midst of Washington, DC metropolitan traffic. Canceling my meetings didn't seem to be an option either as it took an act of God to get people together due to their schedules. Trying to reschedule would require more divine intervention.

I took a deep breath, exhaled, and thought to myself, "Well, that's that. I'll just have to spend the morning's back-to-back meetings in the only clothes I've got: my form-fitting workout shorts and T-shirt." "Taking our casual dress code pretty seriously, aren't we, Mary?" was one of the many teasing comments I would suffer through that morning.

In this high-tech sea of relaxed-fitting chinos, my skin-tight Lycra shorts were transmitting data I would have far preferred to keep to myself. Fortunately, the T-shirt was just long enough to cover the rear view. Its words followed me around all morning: Life is short, learn fast. Life is short, learn fast. Life is short, learn fast. You don't normally expect to get revolutionary messages from any old T-shirt you grab from a drawer in a morning so busy you forget the rest of your clothes. But this one struck me right between the eyes.

It began a new line of information input that just wouldn't give up over the next several weeks, like those electronic news headlines that crawl around buildings in Times Square, only this one was going on in my head:

> *Life's short, learn fast...You're losing concentration...*
> *You're burning out...You're forgetting your pants...*
> *Something has to change...Something has to give...*
> *Life's short, learn fast.*

I had been with America Online for 10 years, helping it drive one of the most historic, explosive business and economic growth periods in history. And now it was time for me to go. It meant that I would be walking away from thousands of dollars in stock options. But to stay would mean an outcome even more unthinkable.

I would depart as AOL's first corporate training manager. I had helped AOL define the characteristics and skills required from managers to achieve its unparalleled place in world corporate affairs and, more importantly, in the daily lives of millions of its members. I would also depart as the company's youngest female call center manager responsible for 250 people who helped millions of members hook up for the first time to the online world.

The company was my home, its employees were like family, and it was where I grew up. AOL was where I discovered what it means to be a key player in a project that would truly change the world, a project that had meaning. AOL was my professional family of origin.

As with any family of origin, to grow you have to go. And so I resigned.

Resigning wasn't the first bodacious thing I did in my young life as a New Economy player, and it wouldn't be the last bodacious thing I did either. But it was the moment that I saw bodaciousness for what it is: The key to thriving in an ever-changing economy that challenges us all to be bigger, bolder, and better, and to have the courage and inner strength to be the best authentic versions of ourselves we can be.

I learned what it means to be bodacious from the most bodacious start-up of the high-tech era. But in order to reach my next level of success and authenticity, I had to find my future elsewhere.

Some Computer Company

Today, AOL and I are both unrecognizable from the versions we were when we first met. Our paths crossed at similar stages in our lives. We were both basically young adults with some existing achievement on our records already. I had an engineering degree from Virginia Tech, but I had already decided I didn't want to use it. While I was in school, AOL was operating as Quantum Computer Services, providing very limited online services to a small group of Commodore 64 computer owners, services such as games, chat rooms, e-mail, and bulletin boards. Management already knew those days were numbered. We were both poised for radical change (although I bet AOL CEO Steve Case had a better idea where he wanted to take the company than I had about my future). For both of us, what had happened in our immediate past was nothing like what was in store. We were both in for the ride of our lives.

We were in the same boat in other ways, too. We both started out hoping that what we were doing would eventually be considered valuable. We both started out sharing space with others: AOL (I mean, Quantum Computer Services) shared its building with a defense consulting company (which, I'm sure was making far more money in those days than AOL was). I would share my first home with four other women, all of us finding our way in the Big City of greater Washington, DC. AOL and I both learned to pay no attention to the criticisms and threats from antagonists who pretended they were supportive but who eventually revealed their true objectives; to dominate us through fear and devaluation. We would both change our names. Only I would change my name back again.

We would both learn what it means to succeed, transforming ourselves beyond anyone's wildest imaginings. AOL would emerge as the world's largest Internet service provider and now owner of HBO, CNN, *Time* magazine, even Looney Tunes, among the vast number of businesses it absorbed by the merger with Time Warner. And a decade after taking an eight-dollar-an-hour customer service representative position, I would emerge from the experience a multi-millionaire with the power and desire to help other women fulfill their career dreams.

But my first ambitions were decidedly more immediate and self-focused. A freshly hatched college grad in 1988, I drove up to Northern Virginia from my small home town of Williamsburg in my parent's Ford Taurus, which they insisted on because they didn't trust my used Escort to have the necessary pep to keep me alive on the notorious Capital Beltway. I already had a possible room lined up in a group house. All I needed was a job, any job, as long as it paid the bills and allowed me time to look around for something better. All I knew was I didn't want to turn my hard –

won degree into an engineering career (much to the dismay of my parents). I could have started making the big bucks right away if I had stuck with engineering. I had no idea what I wanted, not exactly the mark of an educated young woman destined for greatness, in fact, pretty darned pitiful by all external measures.

I was glad to be heading north to the DC area. Over the weeks immediately after my graduation, my mother had become increasingly antsy about my finding work – or rather, my *not* finding work. Life in Williamsburg didn't hold much promise for a new grad unless I wanted to put on a farthingale and guide people around colonial mansions in the historic district or button up a dirndl and help Busch Garden visitors pretend they were in the Old Country. I knew I needed to go to a big metropolitan area to discover what I didn't even know to look for yet.

It was in the *Washington Post* that I saw the ad for customer service representatives for a computer company. It looked moderately tolerable and interesting, so I called the number. And called again. And called again. No one responded to my messages. I could have interpreted that as indifference, taken it personally, and stopped trying. I decided to call one last time. This time I got through and got an appointment for an interview.

I had two interviews that swampy July day, one with a temporary help company and one with Quantum Computer Services, who placed the ad. I was dressed for success. In fact, I thought I looked pretty darn with it in my blue and white seersucker suit, pantyhose, dark blue pumps, matching post earrings, white linen blouse, and a black vinyl portfolio I bought especially for the occasion because I thought it would make me more professional.

The ladies at the temp agency said, "Thanks, we'll call you." But, even as I walked out the door, I knew they wouldn't. I was a miserable failure at every single typing, filing, dictation, and grammar test they put in front of me. A degree in industrial engineering does not prepare you to be quality office help.

Cindy at Quantum said, "Can you start July 11th?" And with my response I took my place among the ranks of only a few people who were pouring the foundations for what would eventually become known as the New Economy.

At eight dollars an hour, and at the lowest possible rank in this company, I figured, "Good, I have a job. Now I can get started in *something*."

My parents told their friends, "Our daughter works in customer service for some computer company."

Where the Boys Are

As one of the few women entering the workforce with a high-tech company (however lowly my job was), and as a daughter of the so-called post-feminist era, I didn't give much thought to women's workplace issues. Even the fact that the call center management was nicknamed the "All Men's Club" didn't bother me. I was just glad to be in this adrenaline-charged environment where so much creativity, vision, and innovation was being harnessed into this thing called online services. There were women in powerful leadership roles, so I believed I had upward mobility. I was just glad to be able to be part of this really cool mission! I rose quickly through the ranks with rapid raises and promotions. I was given the chance time and again to take on responsibilities that were completely new to me. With a few exceptions, I felt treated fairly and acknowledged regularly for my contributions.

I still had such a long way to go before I scraped the proverbial glass ceiling, and it didn't really register with me that year after year after year, the highest executive ranks held hardly any women at all. My gifts for being upbeat, effective, productive, and good at communication and building teams were all gifts commonly associated with female roles. I was rewarded well for helping others. But after 10 years, my career at AOL came to a dead stop with one word; strategic. I wasn't strategic enough, I was told by my boss, who otherwise often told me how indispensable I was.

I didn't remember this criticism ever coming up in my performance appraisals. Becoming more strategic was never factored into any career management plan or objectives that my boss and I had agreed upon. But with that one word, gone was my next best hope for the promotion within the department I deeply wanted. Gone was my lovely office, which I had to relinquish to the man who would be hired from the outside for that position. And gone was my belief that my future was at AOL.

I wasn't "ready," my boss said, to take on the role of director. But I suspect that it was my boss who wasn't ready to perceive me with the formal title officially acknowledging the responsibilities I was already shouldering. And this was before the no-pants episode. In truth, I was being more strategic than he would ever know. Over the years, I helped AOL pump knowledge, motivation, and leadership skills into thousands of its employees as it became a major player in everyday America. All the while I was strategically surviving a marriage that made me feel devalued, controlled, and afraid. Within a few months of our little "strategy" conversation, I had strategically designed a way I could safely leave my husband for the second and final time – a plan that involved a joint meeting with our therapist, a waiting friend, and my car already packed with necessary belongings. You want strategy? I was strategy personified.

I was bodaciousness personified. I had come a long way, I had left a lot behind me, and now it seemed that my last departure would be from the company I had invested so many years and so much passion in. I had also joined the ranks of workplace statistics at this point; the statistics of ambitious women whose value to their companies is lost and whose careers risk being derailed by the failure to accurately capture the true value of their contributions and potential.

With all this talk about an America that's available for anyone with drive and a good business sense, many women still aren't major players in the corporate world. Certainly, we are much better off than we were 30 years ago, but we still have a long way to go. Consider this fact: Women are still paid just 85% (sometimes less) of what men are paid for the same job.

How can that be? Discrimination laws are in place to fight such issues as pay inequities. We have plenty of how-to books giving us the skill sets of negotiating, playing office politics, and "winning at the boys' game". Are we just not listening? Or do we detest the basic message that you must overcome the fact that you're female? Then there are books on work/life balance, still written primarily for women, which continue to put on our shoulders the responsibility of how much of ourselves we're willing to trade for the sake of career, romantic love, dependent children or aging parents.

How are many women being treated in the economy? Like outsiders who are invited to play only if we can somehow find a way to fit in. Yes, there are indeed a number of women who have achieved extraordinary business success. As of this writing, Carly Fiorina is still in charge of Hewlett-Packard. But we know this only because it's so extraordinary that the media have pointed it out to us, "See? Look, there are skirts in the executive suite." There are excellent groups such as American Business Women's Association (www.abwahq.com) and Women in Technology, Inc. (www.witi.org) that are dedicated to encouraging women to play big and aim high. Wouldn't it be nice if we didn't really need them anymore?

The environment is not exactly hostile to women. Of course, there are male decision-makers in power that just can't wrap their brains around the notion of women being leaders and participants in powerful organizations. But for the most part, I'd say it's still a neglectful environment, rolling like that ball in the Indiana Jones movie along a track with no particular thought about the presence and participation of women in high-reward careers.

Is this something to get furious about? Well, you can, if you want. But that's wasting precious time and energy. Don't get mad, get bodacious!

We will finally achieve our bodaciousness tipping point when *Fortune* magazine publishes its last ever annual list of Top Women in Business and we all ask, "So what?" I'm sure that most of the women on this year's list have done so already. Let's join them, shall we?

That's a Good Girl

In a way, it would be better if we were dealing with an openly hostile environment because it's easier to see, and it's just plain illegal. And we could fight that. But we are surrounded by well-meaning men and women who sincerely respect us but yet truly don't see women in the any real position of power as strategic players in the chase for commercial competitiveness. Both men and women both have been culturally encoded to look elsewhere for power and profitable effectiveness on the corporate scene. As women, we have been culturally encoded to set aside our personal power, drive, energy and our fullest authenticity in the name of being nice good and accommodating girls. We're sent messages every day that this is really a man's world and that we may be allowed to participate only if we mind our manners. Yes, we've made huge strides and achievements, but still many of us feel as though we're living a Ladies Night at an exclusive men's club, a special dispensation that might continue as long as the members find it expedient and amusing.

We don't feel this way all the time, but most of us feel that extra pressure every now and then. And in the process, we're made to feel suspicious about each other. I think almost all of us have heard someone say, "No one's harder on women in business than women." I haven't seen any statistic supporting that, have you? It's not been my personal experience. But I also haven't heard anyone speak up and say, "What a crock!" Well here's my vote.

Let's take a look at some of the commercials that reflect what our culture considers acceptable:

- A little girl no older than ten talks confidently to adults about how she takes care of her big brother's hankering for a fruit drink. I would like to suggest the bodacious alternative: "Sure you can have some, Billy. Packets are in the cupboard, pitcher's on the shelf, spoon's in the drawer, water's in the faucet. Knock yourself out."

- A secretary (we assume) is on the phone with Big Boss ("Sir"), reporting that the staff is out, stuck in traffic, at a doctor's appointment, and so on. The boss says, "Isn't there anyone there who knows how much business can be done before 8 A.M.?" "Sure," she says, and hands the receiver to the UPS man. The bodacious alternative: "Sure. You're talking to her. Let's talk about me taking on more responsibility."

- A businesswoman hollers out, "That's my cab!" just as a businessman reaches for the car door handle. Good for her! But then in a higher, appeasing voice she asks, "Share the cab with me?" His response: "Sure, why not!" like he's doing her some kind of a favor. The bodacious alternative – spoken in an comfortable, confident tone: "If we're going the same way, you're welcome to share the cab with me." Notice the statement form and the condition to the offer. And the bodacious man would respond, "That's generous of you. I'd appreciate it."

Why make such a big deal about such trivial things as commercials? Am I saying women of the 21st century are being dominated by diabolical advertisers who conspire against them in walnut-paneled offices high above Madison Avenue? No, of course not. But what is significant about these examples is that they are the product of some of the best creative minds in the country, they've been exhaustively run by focus groups of ordinary people, and evidently no one thought there was anything wrong with them!

We all know better than to interpret any kind of commercial as the absolute truth. But they must ring true on some visceral level in order to effectively convert viewers into buyers. This is where these commercials reflect the deep-seated, culturally encoded assumptions of how women are expected to behave, especially in the context of our relationship with others. "We should put the needs of others before our own." "If our boss undervalues our work, then we must assume our work has little value." "We must value the care and nurturing over anything else, even it means getting into a car with a stranger."

What it all boils down to is this one simple message: Be perfect. Be a good girl. Be nice. Don't offend. Do whatever you need to do to keep relationships intact because they can all fall apart around you with one slip of selfishness. Then you'll be left with nothing but the blame you so richly deserve.

For most American women, the burden is in the accumulated nicks and cuts in our careers and private lives. An acquaintance asks us for an outrageous and imposing favor and we can't say no. We've discovered that our paycheck isn't as much as our male counterpart's and we assume we haven't worked hard enough. We're not included in an important social occasion with our male colleagues and customers. It's time for women to finally throw off the good girl norms that no longer help us. It's time for women to insist that the business world is our world, not one for men alone. It's time for women to bodaciously build the careers they want!

Why "Now?"

I expect that we'll come to regard the New Economy as a transitory period between the Old Economy (that is every market condition that existed before the Internet, other amazing technology, and globalization) and the long stretch ahead of us that I call the Now Economy. The future is hard to predict. We plan as wisely as we can, always watching for what emerges and doing our best to be prepared to respond. One change of circumstances or course of events, even a seemingly small or isolated one, can have a huge effect and cause us all to change once again. "What makes sense now?" is the question we have to keep asking ourselves. Regardless of our specific answer, the goal remains the same; to be relevant and effective so we can not only survive but also thrive and reach our greatest potential.

Reading the memoirs of Bill Gates, Michael Dell or Andy Grove is great, but not enough, unless you want to launch your own Microsoft, Dell Computers or Intel company. Maybe you don't have the drive to take computers apart and build them back up again in your garage or basement. Maybe the word mogul and the "your picture here" silhouette just never seem right together. Maybe leadership on such a gladiator scale just doesn't interest you. It's just not real life to most people in this universe.

However, bodaciousness is within our reach no matter who we are.

To be a bodacious Now Economy player, we'd all do better to take our lessons and inspirations from Now Economy companies and from the stories of the thousands of ordinary civilians, like me, who huffed and puffed and breathed life into these amazing life-changing, world-rearranging organizations. We had to be prepared to do battle as start-ups ourselves before we could expect to bring little Quantum Computer Services forward and launch it into the stratosphere as AOL, with its millions of members and its megalithic media impact.

You may be a fan of AOL or you may detest it, but there's no denying the impact that it has had on the U.S. culture and the way Americans spend their time. Taking a small company serving mostly techno-geeks, professors, and nerds and transforming it into a national living room where Grandpa can sit at his computer and watch a video clip of Billy sing, "Little Bunny Foo Foo," took a lot of long hours, a lot of vision, a lot of spine, and massive bodaciousness from all AOL employees, not just cover boys like CEO Steve Case or COO Robert Pittman.

The Now Economy will be like nothing we've ever seen before. And it will be bodacious people who will enjoy the ride.

Failure is not Trying

If you're feeling a sense of greater risk and peril, you're right. The more you reach for, the more you stand to gain – and lose. Rather, fortunately, you have more to lose. The name of the game is to have more; more confidence, more joie de vivre, more ways to express your authenticity, and, of course, more financial security. Failure in the Now Economy is not going for it, not trying to be all you can be and not attempting to achieve all that you want. Failure is letting your fears keep you back.

Consider the New Testament story of the master, servants, and talents. The master was leaving for a long trip, so he decided to entrust a few of his servants with his property while he was gone. He gave one guy five talents (originally a large amount of money, now more symbolic of abilities), one guy two talents, and the last guy just one talent.

The first two servants went out and used their money to make more money, which involved some risk, I'm sure. Each doubled his lot. The last guy was so scared of losing the single talent that he buried it until the owner came home. Upon his return, the master was thrilled with the two servants who successfully doubled the money and gave them great big rewards. However, he was infuriated with the servant who took no chances with what he had. Staying on par wasn't good enough; the master expected growth and development. Then, talk about a pink slip. The guy was told he was worthless and was thrown out into the "darkness, where there will be weeping and gnashing of teeth." Ouch!

I don't think the master was a particularly nasty guy. He just thought that not proactively using what you have was a crime and that being scared was no excuse. The two other servants had their share of shaking in their boots but took action anyway. The master and his two remaining servants would kick butt in today's Now Economy.

The Trip to Bodaciousness

Bodacious! "Is that even a word?" Yes, it's actually in the dictionary. It means bold, outstanding, remarkable, audacious. It started as a southern term. Can't you just hear the hillbillies? Then there's the testosterone-enriched saying "bodacious ta-tas". I bet you don't need a translation to understand the meaning. It's also a great word for women to claim for themselves: It brings up a vigorous feeling of being courageous, creative and self-respecting while being completely, thoroughly, full-speed-ahead, knowing exactly who you are and relishing the entire experience, without apology.

Although I would never say that a single word changed my life, I can say that bodacious became my own personal rallying cry; three little syllables whose spirit continues to help me create a life that is leading to an even greater sense of who I can be and what I can do.

When I look in the mirror, I see someone like no one I have ever seen before. I see someone who benefited from the 1990s New Economy in amazing ways. I also see someone who is no longer afraid. I'm no longer afraid of my own abilities. I'm no longer afraid of my own confidence. I'm no longer afraid of people thinking I'm not a good girl. I'm not afraid of letting my vulnerabilities show, if and when I choose. I'm no longer afraid of showing my power, experience, and expertise. Best of all, I'm not afraid of what people will think of me as I step forward into full bodaciousness!

Building a Bodacious Career

The wonderful thing about building a Bodacious Career in the Now Economy is that it presents so much possibility if we have the courage to define who we want to be. This same level of possibility presents no firm ground, no firm rules, and therefore lots of opportunity for both success and failure. Our personal risk tolerance is tested and challenged over and over again.

To take that challenge again and again, you've got to be willing to walk the bodacious way. After the first heavy push, the going will be easier with each new challenge. First some foundation work must be laid. You must interact in the workplace with new skills. This is where this book will help.

In these chapters, I will impart my big career lessons from my AOL experience. Imagine we're having a conversation and a few laughs over coffee as I share with you:

- **How to create and use your relationships to help you**

- **When and how to take a stand at work**

- **How to thrive on the Now Economy's constant shift and change**

- **What office politics really are and how to engage in them productively**

- **How to create your personal business plan to build the Bodacious Career you want**

There's plenty of practical advice mixed with inspiration. Each chapter starts with questions for you to consider when building your Bodacious Career and ends with specific actions to take. Check out the dozen side bars for additional ideas onspecial topics, including my Bonus Insert at the end of Chapter Four, *Thrive on Shift and Change,* which covers surviving a layoff and rebounding into a new position.

In companies, both high – and low-tech, there are millions of women throughout the United States and the world wanting more career satisfaction. Today's environment makes that possible now more than ever. You can start any time to build the Bodacious Career you want. But right now would be a really good idea!

Create Deliberate Relationships

In Building Your Bodacious Career...

- Are relationships a big deal?
- Do you deliberately create relationships that matter?
- Is networking the last thing you want to do?
- Do you know how to leverage your relationships for your Bodacious Career?

It's All About Relationships

It didn't take me long after starting at AOL to realize that I was surrounded by a world for which Williamsburg childhood had not prepared me. I wasn't exactly a country bumpkin when I reported for work the first day, but let's face it, my matching blue pumps and "professional" vinyl folder would only take me as far as the interview. After that, it didn't matter whether I was dressed for success or not. The name of the game was doing the job – and, as I soon realized, to get to know people – lots of people.

AOL wasn't the corporate America I'd heard about. My expectation was of men dressed in dark suits and white shirts with neck-choking ties and women basically the same only with foot-aching pumps. It was the late 80s, and this still was reality for many Dilbert-like companies, but certainly not the one I'd joined. In fact, over the years when I did wear anything much dressier than jeans, and especially if I donned a suit, I'd get playfully harassed. "All dressed up today, Mary! When's the interview?" No, my co-workers taught me diversity first hand. We were a motley lot. Tattoos appeared under short sleeves, and earrings hung from places I didn't even know could be pierced. There were the usual computer geeks who couldn't coordinate colors but at least they changed their clothes. And then there were folks who dabbled in trying the latest trends. I remember one time when I felt particularly edgy wearing acid-washed red and black jeans after I'd gotten a daring, new wave hair cut to match.

We must have been a sight for conservative types who shared our building. While in the elevator with some of them, I imagined a cartoon speech balloon over their heads saying, "Who *are* you people?" I fantasized answering, "We may look like riffraff, but we're having the time of our lives creating an online experience you've never seen before."

All my AOL coworkers stood just as good a chance as I did to do well. They were hired for their passion for the online tech world, for what they knew, for what they could learn, and more importantly, what they could do for this bodacious little company with a vision that was already way too big for its britches. As ragtag as we all were, each one of us was carefully interviewed, tested and selected. Now it was up to us to make good. As the weeks passed, we became congealed by that spark, excitement, and passion that would make this really cool dream actually come true.

What I didn't know, and was too unsophisticated to really care, was that AOL's senior leadership, also ragtag in its own way, felt the shared passion of building what would eventually be AOL. In the early days of the company's incarnation, long before AOL was even a glimmer, Dan Case, who was known as an aggressive investment banker from San Francisco, used a very familiar relationship to further the business. It was he who brought in younger brother Steve, an assistant brand manager for Procter & Gamble. Sure, Steve had to have the goods, but a lot of people have the goods – and they don't get to be part of a bodacious start-up unless they have the goods and relationships. It was relationship that put Steve on the track to hard work, fame, and fortune, with a lot of hard work, of course.

I knew none of this when I started. I mean the boss is the boss, right? Who cares how he got there? By the time I started, all the big ideas that had been hatched over dinner meetings, on barstools, and while gazing into computer screens had morphed into Quantum Computer Services, and would later morph again into AOL. Although we all took differing career roads to get here, one thing would keep us coming back (besides the paycheck, of course): Relationships – relationships with the dream and each other. Although we were still more than seven years away from the "official" start of the New Economy (1995, when Netscape went public), we were already building what was needed to thrive in all future economic eras; the business of cultivating and sustaining relationships.

Today's Now Economy is a relationship economy. Everything is introduced, evaluated, negotiated, bought, sold, resolved, ended, and enjoyed based on relationships. Value lies in relationships. Relationships among people form communities, which is why Steve Case was always so big on the AOL service being a community. When people are plugged in (literally) and have a connection with other people as well as information that matters to them, they don't want to leave. However, if the relationship changes for the worse, they may make another choice. Relationships are always in flux and must always be managed.

Bodacious Career builders know that the Now Economy is about using a multitude of pathways to connect with people. The technological advancements that have evolved over recent years serve as both metaphors and evidence of our demand for an infinite ability to make connections through computers, modems, phone lines, and air waves, as well as among people in organizations. Even with all this high-tech stuff, it's still all about people. The hope for the Now Economy lies in the creative breakthroughs people make with technology, not the technology itself. Without the divine spark that only humans can provide, we just have a bunch of computers bleeping on tables in empty rooms. It's the divine spark that drives the technology forward and helps us create the kinds of wonderful products, services, and relationships we have never seen before.

Your Mother Always Said Choose Your Friends Wisely

What I'm about to say here flies in the face of all good girl coding most of us have had embedded in our systems from the day we first heard, "Now play nice. That's a good girl." And it might make you so mad that it will cause you to slam the book shut and put it down forever. I certainly hope not. But in the name of authenticity and full disclosure, I have to tell it like I see it from inside the process: *To build a Bodacious Career, deliberately seek relationships with people according to who they are, who they know, what they do – and what they can do for you.*

Sounds horribly selective, doesn't it? But it isn't really. In fact, I'm sure you already do this. Now it's time to do it strategically. As you move toward a more authentic, bodacious sense of who you are and who you want to be, you're going to want to seek out other Bodacious Women and men whose skills, talents, and contacts compliment your own. And they, in turn, are going to be wondering how to meet a woman like you! This will make your inner good girl feel better; you're actually doing *them* a favor as well.

Why does it sound wicked to be deliberate about selecting and nurturing some friends and ignoring opportunities for other acquaintances? Our good girl coding tells us that friendships are precious gifts we should cherish, no matter where they come from. And that's true. But our coding goes on to say that any strategy on our part is scheming, cold-hearted, and socially materialistic. We're culturally instructed to welcome and nurture almost anyone who enters our sphere, and to do otherwise would be unkind and almost "unwomanly".

So what am I saying, that you should summarily ditch dear friends? Of course not! That would be tragic and cruel! Genuine, sincere, dear friends come in all forms. Your childhood friend with whom you may have nothing in common with at this stage of your life, may still be as much a sister to you as she was before you started this new journey to your bigger, bolder, more audacious self.

But I would like to suggest two ideas:

1. Proactively create relationships with people who can support your own growth, who can contribute meaningfully to your journey. Do the same in return.

2. Realize that as you manifest some of the changes you want to create in your life, you will discover that some of the people you had once called loyal friends were really just acquaintanceships of convenience. And that's okay. Those relationships have their time, purpose, and place, and they're beneficial to both of you. But to expect more from these relationships could be frustrating and even painful.

Bodacious friends are generally positive and optimistic; supportive and encouraging; adventurous in their own bodaciousness process; generous in their positive wishes for you; curious, creative and resourceful, and surrounded by other bodacious friends they want you to meet. They treat themselves kindly and take petty emergencies and disappointments lightly. They can be needful at times but they are never chronically needy. Bodacious friends allow others to be themselves.

Relationships to keep at arm's length are people who are jealous and resentful of your good news, they make you feel uneasy, defensive or tense. You find yourself focusing only on negative situations or complaints when you talk to these people. These people make you feel sheepish, selfish or ashamed of your own personal growth process because they are more invested in sustaining their pain than learning about new worlds, new options, and new possibilities.

How can you get more of one kind of relationships and less of the other? Think like a bodacious business and do what Now Economy recruiters are doing to attract top-notch talent.

Strategies for Staffing Your Bodacious Career

Think of how you've created relationships at work in the past. My guess is that more often than not, you've created friendships based on those around you who you easily connected with or felt some kinship because of working closely together or having something in common. These approaches are okay, but they don't do much to increase the quality of the selection. This is very much the way Old Economy companies operated their general recruitment programs. Many of these organizations would put an ad in the paper and select among the best applicants who came along, hoping that the "best" was reading the help wanted ads. This Old Economy recruitment technique has huge limitations. These employers aren't tapping into the overall community of potential employees, they are trying to fill specific vacancies for *now* rather than creating a bodacious future for the company.

In contrast, Barbara Beck, senior vice president of the bodacious Cisco Systems, once stated in *Fast Company* magazine that "We don't fill jobs; we're constantly looking for people who can help drive the company forward." A Bodacious Career needs the support of future-oriented and growth-oriented relationships. Do your friends help you drive your Bodacious Career forward? Do they welcome your interest in helping them drive their careers and lives forward? If not, maybe you need to reconsider who you call friends!

You have one huge advantage over Now Economy companies, however. As employers of full-time workers, they are limited as to the availability of their candidates. This is a one-at-a-time-only deal. Once they've plucked a candidate off the market, that person is out of circulation, unavailable to other companies until he or she ready to leave the current employer. If this individual is a high quality, bodacious performer, you can count on the current employer doing everything they can think of to hang on to them. That's what they mean by "war for talent".

Your advantage is that you're not restricted by how many relationships you can have. You can have as many as you want! And you can share them with others. In fact, the more high quality circles we belong to, the better off for everyone. All will benefit from bodacious connections.

So how do you create relationships that matter to your Bodacious Career? Here are some strategies:

STRATEGY 1: PROFILE YOUR IDEAL CANDIDATE

High quality companies have one thing in common: They know that if you aspire to be the best, you seek out the best. You know what they say about birds of a feather. There's a widely understood and accepted principle: Like attracts like, and in order to find what you want, you have to know what you're looking for. That's why there's almost always a description of background requirements with each job description that you see. If you're looking for the *best*, you must decide how you define *best*.

So what kind of people would be best for building your Bodacious Career? Someone with certain experience that you'd like to learn from; someone with organizational rank that you want to make sure knows you exist; someone in another part of the company whose performance goals are linked to yours? I can't dictate the specifics. Only you can decide these things for yourself, according to your values and objectives. While there are no "right" one-size-fits-all answers, here are suggestions of the kinds of people to seek out when looking for bodacious connections:

- people who are in key leadership positions
- women who are successful in your profession
- women who represent an achievement or personal growth spurt that you would like to experience
- professional people who are in a certain age bracket
- people who are in a certain income bracket
- people who are passionate about what they do
- professional people who are active in sports
- people who are enrolled in graduate degrees in your field
- professional people who are members of your church or place of worship
- professional women who are mothers of children the same age as yours

Thinking of developing relationships this way may feel awkward at first, but I encourage you to give it a try. You have nothing to lose but the potential of meeting someone who could make a huge difference to your career. And, remember, when you know who you're looking for, they'll be easier to find.

STRATEGY 2: IDENTIFY WHAT'S IN IT FOR THEM

The main difference between staffing your Bodacious Career and companies looking to hire is that with the companies, a paycheck is usually involved. And it's safe to assume you don't want to pay someone to be your friend, so you have to offer something else of value. Identify what's in it for them to invest their time with you.

This little exercise is important for two reasons:

1. Consciously or unconsciously, people (especially busy, in-demand people) have a tape of discernment running in their heads. With each choice to bring someone new in their lives, they ask themselves, "What's in it for me?" It could be something strictly emotional: "Being around Kate makes me feel inspired." Or it could be something practical and specific, such as your power within an organization or the power of the organization itself, for instance. If you're able to succinctly and gracefully capture what you have to offer, you'll get their attention sooner.

2. By fully appreciating the value of what you have to offer, you neutralize the curse of your own "who am I to contact *her*" feeling of unworthiness. Even making cold calls, which so many people dread, becomes easier when you know you have something of value to offer.

So what do people get from investing their time with you, knowledge of a project or person they didn't know before, introductions to others they'd like to know, ideas that can help them in their role? Come up with a few possibilities. If people show interest, at some point early on, you can ask, "I know we're just getting to know each other, but what are one or two ways that I can help you?" They may or may not have an immediate answer, but you will leave an impression of goodwill and mutual benefit. At the very least, they will have the opportunity to develop a relationship with someone who is upbeat, optimistic, creative, and resourceful.

STRATEGY 3: BE A TALENT SCOUT

Cisco Systems is famous for its unique ways to reach out to high potential candidates. One year, the company sent a group of Cisco employees to a football game between Stanford University and the University of California at Berkeley – both high quality schools with high-performing students and alumni in the high-tech fields. Cisco wasn't taking sides though. They celebrated points scored by either team. At each end zone, the Cisco contingent of employees would wave placards that spelled out www.cisco.com/jobs. On a separate occasion, the company actually set up a booth at the Santa Clara Home and Garden Show, but they weren't looking at expanding the business into horticulture. Cisco reasoned that anyone successful enough to actually own a house and garden in the infamously pricey Silicon Valley area must have been doing something right with his or her career. These were the people Cisco wanted to meet, so their booth was positioned among the trowels, tulips, and turf.

You can borrow inspiration from Cisco's example. The idea is to put yourself where other bodacious people are likely to be. Like Cisco, use your imagination to beef up your Bodacious Career staffing possibilities:

- **Eat in the company cafeteria and sit next to someone you don't know.** Do this with a friend or be really bodacious and do it solo. Or, at a meeting, sit next to someone you don't know. Introduce yourself and start asking them simple questions about what they do or illicit their thoughts about a recent company event. See the section "Take the Work out of Networking" for more ideas on starting conversations with unfamiliar folks.

- **Do more than transact business with a third party to get something done for your company.** Many companies hire or outsource other companies to do a task they can't or don't want to do. Use these built-in relationships for expanding who you know in other companies. Take time to manage these relationships for your immediate needs and future connections. See the sidebar "Use Third Party Relationships for Your Company and Your Career" for more tips on utilizing this valuable relationship resource.

- **Attend professional business meetings in your area.** Most large newspapers feature a local business calendar. You'll find announcements of local chapter meetings, professional associations, seminars, trade shows, etc. Don't just attend, but take time to meet people and get involved.

- **Start a Bodacious Book Club at work, in your neighborhood or with other Bodacious Women.** In particular, read and discuss professional development books or biographies of amazing women.

- **Attend hobby centers of activities that are likely to be frequented by bodacious people.** For instance, attend home and garden events; scuba diving club outings; museum tours; free lectures at your local bookstore, gourmet or natural food store; outdoor community summer concerts or continuing education classes at your local college, especially business classes.

- **Seek out circles of impassioned public service-minded volunteers.** Some of the most bodacious people are in these kinds of mission-driven circles. Their self-esteem is fueled by the hope and the expectation that their efforts will make a difference. It doesn't matter what you volunteer for, as long as you believe in it. It could be Habitat for Humanity, your local humane society, local literacy programs, meals for the house bound or battered women's shelters. There is a place for your passion in public service, and that's where you will develop relationships with equally passionate and energetic people.

Always be on the look out for and open to new relationship opportunities to staff your Bodacious Career. Start with people in your company and profession, then go beyond these obvious circles to ones where you have a common interest. If you have a focus that's not work-related, that can make it easier to start conversations and get to know people.

Side Bar
Use Third Party Relationships for Your Company and Your Career

When it comes to business relationships with third parties, you may be thinking, "Why should I put any real effort into creating a good relationship with the company I hired to make my workload easier?" Answer: Because you'll get the most effective result possible for your company and because these are potential relationships for building your Bodacious Career. Here are some things I did at AOL that worked well in maximizing third party potential:

- **Think of the third party provider as a partner, not a vendor:** A vendor relationship makes it merely a transaction. It's like buying toothpaste: You need it and pay for it, but you're not very involved. Being a partner means treating the other party with respect like you would any peer who thinks beyond the basic exchange and considers what the other person needs to be successful.

- **Express your expectations clearly:** Be as specific as possible. What are the deliverables? What's the time line? What behaviors do you want? Let the other party know what success looks like to you. That way, they can target their efforts and you will have something to measure their performance.

- **Be willing to share information as much as possible:** Certainly it takes time to feel comfortable exchanging sensitive company information. Give your partner as much as you can. Remember, partners aren't miracle workers. They need the same raw material as you.

- **Give feedback often:** Be specific about what's going well and what concerns you. If they're worth their salt, they'll keep doing what you like and change what you don't.

- **Spend time getting to know partners and their businesses:** Ask them out for lunch or coffee, ask them about how their career developed, and introduce them to others within the company or another company who may find their work useful. Show interest in those they introduce to you.

- **If a major change happens, tell partners as soon as you can:** Ever changing circumstances are the norm of the Now Economy. When a change occurs, let your partners know so they can adjust. Sometimes it means

their work is done. If so, treat them with respect. Keep in touch with them even if you are no longer actively working together. You never know when you'll need them again.
In short, don't burn bridges.

STRATEGY 4: CREATE RECRUITMENT EVENTS

It used to be that if you drove north on Highway 101 from just south of San Jose to San Francisco, you were taking part in a huge recruitment event. The highway was lined on both sides with come-ons from companies with jobs they needed to fill. There were billboards stacked up along 50 miles of highway, and banners hung from the windows of ultra-modern, high-tech office buildings. There was also a company who regularly leased the Santa Clara Convention Center and hosted hundreds of companies who were recruiting highly desirable, technically-skilled talent in the Silicon Valley.

Today the job market is much tighter and companies aren't recruiting as aggressively. But that doesn't mean they'll settle for warm bodies to fill positions. They want extremely qualified people who are the right match for their organization. It's the same for building relationships for our Bodacious Career. With all of the infinite possibilities that are available to companies and to us for making valuable matches, we all still struggle with the same old challenge: How do we make meaningful connections? Once again, look at what the pros do: Hold recruitment events. But instead of seeking to hire these people, your objective is to expand your wealth of contacts. You don't even have to worry about "placing" them in any particular "jobs" or "assignments". This isn't about making ractical use of people you meet. It's about strategically collecting equally bodacious people for future possibilities. Here are some simple recruitment ideas:

• **Where two or more are gathered together...it's probably in the workplace kitchen or break room:** Simply going in for your second cup of coffee can be a recruitment event. The coffee station is one of the places you're likely to encounter a powerful, key player from another department. As you pour your coffee, do you stare at the pot and meagerly grumble a greeting that basically translates into, "Uh, you're in the way of the Sweet and Low?" A more outgoing, friendly, "Hi, how are ya? I'm Linda" could be the first step toward a fascinating new project, connection, idea or social circle. Get a conversation rolling, even if it's a short one, just smile and stir in your half-and-half. It could make a huge difference to your future.

• **Create a women's leadership discussion group at work.** Invite other women in your company to gather once or twice a month to discuss various aspects of your profession, industry or company directions. Keep the conversation business and career-oriented, especially if you hold the meetings on company property. Again, the emphasis is on building positive, creative, resourceful discussions about the business that will move everyone forward in their careers. Don't let discussions dissolve into a complaint fest.

• **If you're not sure an ongoing discussion group will fly, try a one-time event to test interest.** I did that once at AOL when I worked in the human resources department. During one summer, it seemed to me I was having similar conversations with my female human resources (HR) colleagues who were spread out among half a dozen business units. My sense was that if we could all get together, we'd begin to find support and solutions to our challenges at work. So I put together a chili and pool

"HR Female Thang" outing. (The last thing we needed was to sit around eating and complaining. A little out-of-the-ordinary recreation creates a common, fun experience and gets the creative juices flowing.) I personally benefited by establishing a friendship with a Bodacious Woman that otherwise wouldn't have developed.

- **Identify your counterparts outside your immediate company and meet regularly to address common areas of interest and concern.** Perhaps there are a few people in your professional association that you'd like to get to know better. Invite them to meet once a month or quarter at a local coffee shop or for lunch at a centrally located restaurant. Have a few questions to ask, be prepared to share your thoughts as well and see what transpires.

- **Throw a "bring one" party.** Remember what I said about birds of a feather? If you are interested in expanding your network of powerful, positive, creative, upbeat, and resourceful men and women...well, I'm certain you know a few already. And I'm also certain that they know even more bodacious people from other business and social circles. Plan a party at your home or a local gathering place and invite all the bodacious people you know. Ask each person to bring a bodacious friend or significant other. At this gathering, have each person introduce him or herself, identifying what they're passionate about, what their special talent is, what they're working on, and what kind of help they need or information source they could use.

Side Bar

10 Things You Want Your Reputation to Say About You

Career bodaciousness is developing a reputation for being smart, focused on what's good for the business, optimistic and well respected throughout the company and the larger marketplace. Unless you have a good reputation, you won't have the bodacious relationships you'll need to thrive to your fullest potential in the Now Economy environment. Here are ten things you want your reputation to say about you to set you up for Bodacious Career building:

1. **Give credit where it's due.** In the Now Economy, you're nothing without the support of other peoples' contributions, technical know-how, and creative ideas. Make sure you share the credit with your team members, and let them know you did.

2. **Create a safe place for brainstorming.** People need to know you'll receive their ideas in a respectful and kind manner. Assure them you believe there is really no such thing as a bad idea and that you are open to all possibilities.

3. **Respect yourself and take yourself lightly too.** Your self-respect will elicit respect from others. Your ability to laugh at your own moments of foolishness or mistakes will make everyone relax around you. (Just be mindful that not all your comments are self-deprecating. That's a sign that you don't think much of yourself, which, if you're bodacious, isn't true.)

4. **Keep confidences.** As you move up in an organization, colleagues and employees may share intimate, personal information about themselves with you. You may also be privileged to certain company secrets. Make sure you remain discreet and people will continue sharing valuable information with you.

5. **Seek out diversity.** High-potential employees and friends are found among every age, class, race, sex, level of education, and organizational position. Create space in your life that will hold anyone of caliber.

6. **Be comfortable with conflict.** You may not love it, but you need to accept that conflict is a dynamic circumstance that can lead to even more powerful creativity. Don't lose your cool or get mean when the heat's on.

7. **Share information.** Share "public domain" information from your department or other parts of the business that will help others. Pass on interesting articles, books, and observations to help others grow in their own careers and lives.

8. **Try to assume the positive in a questionable circumstance.** When you're in doubt, you can go one of two ways: pessimistic and suspicious or optimistic and positive. People will feel safe with you if they know you're thinking the best of them. This doesn't mean you give up your discernment. If someone's dealings seem shady, you're best to distance yourself from them, at least until you know more.

9. **Don't inflate negative situations.** Sure bad things happen,but try to keep them in perspective.

10. **Don't appear doubtful about your principles.** When you put a stake in the ground, mean it. Take a stand.

Take the Work out of Networking

While you're trying out one or more of my strategies for staffing your Bodacious Career, you're going to come smack up against your like or dislike of networking. I find that women either love it or hate it. When they love it, they truly enjoy meeting others and are great at it. When they hate it, they'd rather go get a mammogram. At least in that situation, no one expects you to do more than stand there. Knowing how to network well can make or break your career. That's how powerful it is, because that's how powerful relationships are to your career.

I'm not keen on the term "networking". The problem is the word "work". I mean how many times do you walk into a room full of people expecting to leave with actual work in hand such as a signed contract? It doesn't happen! Why? Because before someone signs their name or hands over a check, there's lots of getting to understand each other, lots of exchange, and making a connection. So, I say we rename "networking" to "netconnecting". Meeting and getting to know new people is about gathering – netting – several good connections. Once you've connected, sharing business cards is simply the convenience of not having to write down their contact information on a napkin.

Today, people who know me have a very hard time believing I was very shy as a little girl. One time in first grade, my mouth was shut for so long, my lips dried together! Seriously. I remember prying them open. When I left for college, I was ready to leave home but I was a bit intimidated about meeting lots of people. It wasn't until I had to make small talk with girl after girl at sorority "rush" parties that I became comfortable with talking to people I didn't know. There's something to be said for diving in to overcome your fear and discomfort. What I learned from these early networking experiences is that I made it much more work than it had to be. In fact, it was easier than I thought once I realized something so obvious: People love to talk about themselves, especially when they're nervous! What better thing to do than to ask them about the topic they know best?!

The key to netconnecting is having a few easy, open-ended questions to get people started, and they're off. Something as simple as, "Hi, I'm Mary. Tell me, how do you stay out of trouble during the day?" (Notice I used a humorous way to replace the tired old question, "What do you do?" Humor is a great way to break the ice and put people at ease.) At that point, all you have to do is listen. Often the person will provide information that prompts you to say something like, "That's interesting, tell me more." The best part is they feel good about you because you made them feel good about themselves! Sure, at some point you need to share about yourself, but that'll come after the ice has melted. Most of all, you've created a connection.

The Three 'A's to Leveraging Your Relationships

As you strategically staff your Bodacious Career, you may wonder, "What do I do with all these relationships once I have them?" Here's where it's time to get even more creative. These relationships can be resources for your next best thing.

The difference between winners and losers is that winners reach out to their relationships and start the process of mobilizing their talent and power network. This is a bodacious alternative to thinking that your personal power is defined by the margins of your résumé which outlines a chronological progression of one job or project to the next. By following the examples of successful entrepreneurs and start-up companies, you can extend the boundaries of your résumé and create a multi-dimensional profile of exactly what you're capable of – with a little help from your friends of course.

As important as a great new idea may be, its best chance to be realized comes when you reach out to others. Bring the powerful talents, passions, and finances of other people into the mix, and deliver the product to the marketplace as fast as you can. This is how AOL emerged from a distant third in the online services marketplace (behind Prodigy and CompuServe). At AOL, we didn't try to create everything ourselves, that would have slowed us down intolerably and taken more capital than the company possessed. Instead, we developed alliances with other companies and individuals to provide certain pieces. We acquired other organizations for critical know-how and strategic positioning, and we acted as an aggregator of technology and information content to create an online experience unlike any previously created. We can leverage these same three 'A's in building our Bodacious Careers; alliances, acquisitions, and aggregation.

ALLIANCES

You may not even realize it, but you create and operate within alliances every day. When you go to the dentist, both you and the dentist are in alliance working to keep your teeth healthy. When you go out on a date, you enter into an alliance with another to create a pleasant evening. When you retain a divorce lawyer, you enter into an alliance in which the objective is to make sure your interests are protected while you dissolve a bad match. When you ask your company's graphics department to design a brochure for you, you enter into an alliance to create an attractive, persuasive piece of paper that will help you sell the company's product or service. So now that you're aware of this approach as a mechanism for strategically achieving more powerful objectives, you can riffle through a mental list of bodacious relationships and select the ones most likely to powerfully raise your ideas to the next level.

For example, shortly after AOL announced its acquisition of Netscape in the late 1990s, iPlanet, a three-way alliance among AOL, Netscape and Sun Microsystems was launched. Each party developed Internet-related companies. The idea was to use the unique skills and abilities of each group to offer e-commerce solutions to businesses. Netscape brought its pioneering browser, Sun brought its server technology, and AOL added its content and consumer knowledge. iPlanet became the choice of over half the Fortune 100 companies, including seven of the top 10 commercial banks, nine of the top 10 telecoms, and a half-dozen leading wireless ventures. Now that's a bodacious relationship result!

When it comes to your Bodacious Career, often times the more you move up and take on more responsibility, the more you'll need cooperation from those in other departments. Perhaps it's a cross-departmental project that's key to a new product or service. Perhaps you're responsible for providing certain services to an internal business unit. Such was the case when I was head of corporate training for AOL. The President of the technology division wanted all of his managers to get trained on how to coach employees for improved performance. To get the job done and done well, I had to create multiple alliances with all the VPs, Directors, Managers and Supervisors below the top gun. That's when I really learned the art and science of thinking and acting like a consultant. I approached them with a service mindset, asked a lot of questions to understand their view, and determined what was in it for them. (See the related sidebar "Create Strong Alliances by Thinking like a Consultant".) One time, we successfully delivered training to 400 managers on four training courses in four months. The technology President was thrilled!

Side Bar

Create Strong Alliances by Thinking like a Consultant

Thinking like a consultant keeps you customer oriented, which is the best way to set yourself up for a successful alliance or other relationship inside your company. When it's all about the internal customer, you can bet it's really all about results. Here are a few techniques I learned during my AOL days to be an effective internal consultant:

- **Ask good questions, lots of them:** Questions that are specific and pertinent to the situation will garner the best results. You'll need to ask some close-ended "yes or no" questions, but your most valuable questions are the open-ended kind that will lead to an ongoing conversation.

- **Listen, listen, listen:** It's more powerful for consultants to talk less and listen more. You may be thought of as a content expert, but only the internal client can give you the raw situational-specific information to apply your experience. In particular, listen to what's *not being* said. There may be an important reason certain details were left out. Ask more questions. Listen some more.

- **Be clear on what the other person wants:** What are their expectations? They may not be sure, so you may need to help them discover and articulate them. Be specific, because the more specific you are, the more likely you can satisfy their needs – and they'll know it.

- **Be clear and honest about how you can or cannot meet their needs:** This is where integrity matters. Don't say you can do it if you really can't deliver. It's better to not promise certain outcomes than do a poor job. Referring someone who can help will keep the relationship open and intact for something possible in the future.

- **Continuously monitor the customer's satisfaction with your work:** If your internal customer is unhappy with your work in progress, it's likely he or she won't like the end result either. Sometimes they won't tell you directly because of the emotional discomfort, sometimes because they aren't completely aware of themselves. Watch for subtle changes in tone, less frequent communication, exclusion from meetings or anything that's different from their usual behavior toward you.

- **Continuously monitor the landscape for changes:** In addition to what your direct customer thinks, keep tabs on what's going on with other people and the organization. Ideally you can leverage changes to enhance the outcome of your efforts. Worse case scenario is that your efforts are shut down, but hopefully, you will have seen that coming. If that's the situation, don't take it personally. Just move on.

- **Build on your performance:** As you build your relationship and prove your value, build on that success by proposing more ways you can help or work together. Perhaps a change of events will create new opportunities. Be proactive when you point out a problem you think you an solve and suggest how you can provide effective relief.

ACQUISITIONS

When a company engages in an acquisition, they actually acquire or purchase all or part of another company. AOL has participated in many acquisitions, but the two most famous are the purchase of Netscape in 1999 and the monster acquisition of Time Warner in 2001.

I'm assuming you're not interested in slave trade or body parts, so this model doesn't directly fit the relationships aspect of building your career. Or does it? While you certainly can't actually "buy" someone else, you can definitely acquire the skills, knowledge, and insight they have on a particular area you want to master. To me, this is the intrigue behind the reality TV show *The Apprentice* which offered one person the hip-joined, slave driver experience of assisting real estate tycoon Donald Trump. Amidst the good, bad and the ugly, this newbie was getting the education of a lifetime. Often when we think of acquiring knowledge, we think of getting a formal education, attending workshops, reading book, listening to tapes, and so forth. These are good options. But what about people we know or would like to know better? Perhaps you can offer to pay someone to transfer their unique knowledge into your head. Many people are flattered to be asked. Payment doesn't necessarily mean you have to pay money. You can give back by giving some of your time to their project or inviting them to great lunches or dinners.

Here's another tip regarding acquisitions for building your Bodacious Career: If your company role includes hiring, those you select can be the difference between maintaining your current status or pumping you up a notch. Their performance will directly reflect on you and your leadership ability. Carefully choose the best person for the job, give them guidance and feedback, monitor their performance, and take any necessary action if things don't work out. These are all keys to making your acquisition work for both you and the company. If you do this well and consistently get results that matter, you will be perceived as a strategic, effective leader – a major prerequisite for moving into the higher ranks of any organization.

AGGREGATION

The difference between alliance and aggregation is the role of power. With an alliance, two parties combine their assets to create a third value element. They equally share power. In an aggregation, one party is the power linchpin, collecting and organizing all the other contributors. A temp agency, for example, is an aggregator. The owner of the agency collects the best of available temporary skilled employees and offers the combined result to the marketplace.

How can you be an aggregator? Suppose you had a cracker-jack idea for a new service to offer existing customers. This may require pulling together several parts of the company that haven't been combined before. You pitch it to your boss and she decides to give you a shot at making it happen. To do so requires you to tap into several alliances with other groups to go in on the idea. You know your relationship building strategies have worked when the groups gives their approval. As the aggregator, you have the vision, are in charge of what you're creating, and can pull in others to form something new. You successfully launch the new service and customers love it! You've created the opportunity to help the business while demonstrating just how creative, risk-taking and strategic you are. There's no way your boss or your boss' boss wants you to go back to what you were doing before. They've got bigger plans for you!

To Build Your Bodacious Career...

• Determine which relationships benefit your career and which ones aren't helping you move forward. Continue to build positive relationships and minimize your interaction with those who drag you down.

• Decide who in your company could help your career in some way and how you will go about getting to know them better.

• Try at least one strategy for creating new relationships out side of your work environment.

• Compose two or three simple, open-ended questions you can use for netconnecting. Test them out, tweak, and use them often so they feel natural.

• Consider how you can create an alliance, use an acquisition or be an aggregator to grow your career.

Take a Stand

- Are you clear about how you want people to treat you?

- Have you experienced your boundaries being crossed or violated?

- What happens to your self-worth when you don't stick up for yourself?

- Are you ready and willing to take a stand?

- Do you know how to handle someone taking a stand with you?

Listening to the Boundary Channel

Life has a way of teaching us really important lessons in stereo. When you don't pick up a message on one channel – say, in your career – you get an extra review chapter on a second channel, often in another area, like your personal life. The message to slow down, for instance, doesn't only come the morning we sleep past the alarm. It also comes in ever-escalating episodes; your car breaks down, your electricity is cut off – hey, you forgot to pay the bill. While running, you stumble on loose pavement, break your ankle, and end up hobbling on crutches.

One lesson women typically have a difficult time with is establishing boundaries. As little girls, most of us are never taught how to say, "This is what I want." If we're particular about anything, say from the shade of our lipstick to how we want our CDs organized, we're criticized for being picky, selfish or spoiled. Think, for example, how Meg Ryan's character in *When Harry Met Sally* was treated when she asked for her salad or her pie a la mode just so. If people love you, that sort of behavior is endearing or cute, so long as it doesn't embarrass anyone or cause them pain or inconvenience. Everyone else finds it really annoying.

The only time teenage American girls are overtly encouraged to lay down the law is on dates with teenage boys. Heaven forbid if we take up too much room or interrupt someone. We're taught to get out of the way, serve everyone before ourselves, and to be mindful of other people's feelings. Furthermore, we're taught to treat others the way we want to be treated and they'll notice and return the favor. No muss. No fuss. No risk. Right?

In a perfect world, that may be true. But who lives in a perfect world? Setting boundaries is one of the lessons I learned in stereo. Because I grew up in a happy, healthy family where we treated each other respectfully and kindly, I entered my adult life unskilled at standing my ground in moments of conflict. I never had my boundaries or principles violated until I was in my mid-20s. And it wasn't until I started applying at work what I was learning in marital therapy that I truly understood how establishing boundaries and respect can be a problem for most American women, no matter their backgrounds.

I also learned that as a woman steps fully into her personal bodaciousness, she's going to start taking up more space. Boundaries are going to start expanding and she's going to have to protect those boundaries and establish new rules of standards for how she's going to be treated. Yes, boundaries are still an issue, even in the Now Economy. As women, we have more opportunity than ever to be who we want to be. You'd think we would have licked this one already, but it's still a core barrier. Some of us don't have the language or skills to stick up for ourselves. As teenagers, we may have been able to say no in the back of a car, but as adults it's hard to take a stand in our careers or in our personal relationships. We're just not comfortable setting boundaries.

If this chapter was written in the 1970s, I suppose it would have been considered the chapter on assertiveness. If you look up the word in the dictionary, its definition includes *aggressiveness*. But most American girls know there's a big difference. To be assertive is somehow okay, but heaven forbid we should cross the line into aggressiveness. That would be terrible because it would make other people feel bad (or so we assumed). Because of the women's movement, we gained responsibility for getting what we wanted, but we also had to do it in such a way that no one would object to our behavior. We had to do it according to a very precise code that no one really knew the key to.

If we acted in a manner less than lady-like, we still risked being marked as manipulative, conniving or the other b-word. Not many women have actually been called those things out loud, but we all worry about it. We are so afraid to risk a negative reaction that we choose not to take any action at all. And that's where we lose our bodacious power!

Even in the Now Economy, the warning messages of what a terrible reputation we'll develop are far more vivid than any instruction on how to move confidently and effectively inside the work environment. What a hassle! For three decades, working women have said, "I'll just go the good girl route until someone figures this one out." Result? We still make less money than men, we're still underrepresented at the executive and board levels of corporations, and we're still hearing the absurd expression, "It's a man's world."

But it's not. It's *everyone's* world. The Now Economy needs everyone to perform to his or her full potential. But to be able to do this, everyone must feel bodacious enough to say, "This is exactly what I want. And this is what I don't want." This is a lesson we can all learn. If you learn it quickly and learn it well, maybe you will be able to avoid getting it in stereo.

Get Control Over What You Can Control

It was my marriage that sent me into counseling. But it was my career that ultimately benefited from what I learned. I entered into both my career and my marriage completely naïve about how to stand up for myself. Yet I wanted to feel good about myself and my work. Achievement was really the main thing I had focused on since my early adult life. I wanted a happy, healthy marriage, and I wanted excellence on the job. These sound like hopeful expectations that any parent would love their kids to have. There was just one problem: I had an undeveloped ability to deal with conflict. But, as it turned out, so much of my marriage would be about conflict and violated boundaries that I sought professional help to learn how to protect my own well-being while working to keep the marriage alive.

I knew I had to learn to establish expectations throughout all areas of my life, including work. No one at AOL knew what I was coping with at home, and I continued to achieve my goals on the job, which resulted in some very nice promotions. One of the most important steps up for me was taking over as call center manager in 1994, when AOL was poised for hyper-growth. In only fourteen months, the call center would go from 70 customer service representatives and three supervisors to 235 reps and 15 supervisors. They were a motley crowd, and paid the least of AOL employees, but they were also the main contact with our members. We needed to keep them passionate about AOL. I also knew that our departmental hyper-growth was the first puff of a huge explosion within AOL. As we grew, the rest of the company was mushrooming up behind us. Between 1995 and 1999, the company would expand from 1,200 to 12,000 employees. I believed that how we handled the call center hyper-growth was a test of how the company would handle the hyper-growth needed to capture the lead in the online services market. The heat was on.

Remember what I said about learning in stereo? One month after taking the call center manager job, I left my husband for the first time (the boundary lesson would take a second time to really take hold). I had also found the courage to say, "No more." No more harsh criticism, no more unrealistic expectations, no more unfair demands, no more fear. After one particular counseling session, I went home and watched as my husband wound himself up for a fight. Time seemed to go in slow motion as I saw what was about to happen. So I got up and ran, accidentally leaving my keys on the kitchen counter. I knew retrieving them would be a mistake. So feeling like a fugitive, I called a friend from a neighbor's and set about starting my own personal hyper-growth.

I was learning to be the leader of my life, and that fed into learning how to be a leader at work. Work continued to be frantic, nothing stopped just because I was going through a personal crisis. When I had taken over the call center, everything was in chaos. We were constantly adding new customers and growing more quickly than we could handle. As a result, we had more calls and more customer requests than we could easily manage. With added demand, there was added stress. Every day, our reps faced an ongoing stream of calls waiting to be answered. Most of the calls were from tense customers with a question or a problem, impatient after waiting on hold for so long. There was a pervasive feeling throughout the department that we couldn't do anything about it. All we could do, according to department culture, was hire people as fast as we could to replace those who burned out. Funny, but throwing bodies on the problem wasn't working.

So I put my first stake in the ground and did something that would seem so obvious to anyone from the outside but was really a huge culture shift from within: I established standards and insisted we keep them.

I knew we couldn't control everything, but I also knew there were certain aspects of the work that were within our control, even if it meant making our customers stay on hold a few seconds longer. We needed to give people breaks to recharge, we needed to create schedules that handled the workload better, we needed to establish quality and attendance standards, and we needed to invest back into employees by giving them training, one-on-one feedback, and team meetings to keep them informed about company developments.

And we needed to fire those employees who couldn't or wouldn't perform according to standards, the least of which was not showing up to work on time.

At first, people were shocked. We'd had attendance policies before, but they were never enforced, and we'd suffered the consequences. For example, if a call center rep was a mere 15 minutes late to his or her shift, that meant three customer calls went unanswered. If ten people were late, that meant thirty customers were backed up. Once behind, we'd never catch up. So we reintroduced our attendance policies, announcing that we would be tracking attendance and that we were serious this time. When people didn't measure up, we would let them know and give them a warning. But those who couldn't cope were gone before long.

Over a short period of time, this new norm became part of the department's culture. We couldn't afford to lose valuable employees, and we did everything we could to keep them. It was quickly understood that if you got fired, you earned it. Almost right away, the mood of the place changed. There was a higher consistency in work quality. There was more mutual respect and far more camaraderie. People actually liked coming to work and started recommending friends for openings.

Meanwhile, I spent the next year going to counseling and sleeping in the spare bedroom of a friend's townhouse. I was getting control over what I could control, and learning to let go of the rest.

Powerfully Positive

Sometimes the idea of setting up boundaries feels like more trouble than it's worth, doesn't it? I know, a little boundary here, snip snip, a little principle there, snip snip. What's the big deal? Well, after a while, those boundaries add up. You've heard the expression "Nature abhors a vacuum", right? People also rush in to fill up a soft space you might have created by allowing a boundary to get mushy.

Try this experiment the next time you're at a red light. Let your car inch forward just a little bit and keep an eye on the car behind you. It will move forward too. It's nothing to take personally. These folks aren't even thinking. They're just moving along, filling in the space that's left in front of them. Space at the red light is hardly anything to obsess about. But it's a perfect illustration of the principle that if you're not mindful of your physical or emotional boundaries, you'll sacrifice your bodacious margins to others, whether they willfully invade your space or not.

Establishing boundaries requires you to take a stand. Taking a stand at work, however, is not just protective, it's powerfully positive. It's bodacious. Consider these reasons why:

- **Taking a stand demonstrates your self-worth.** By consistently enforcing your boundaries, you are also reminding and reinforcing your sense of self-worth. By allowing even the smallest violations to pass without comment, you're telling yourself and others that your thoughts and feelings aren't as important as theirs. Once that process is set into motion, it's difficult to reverse the trend.

- **Taking a stand establishes trustworthiness.** By delineating your boundaries, you tell people what to expect of you. Not too long after I took over the call center manager position, I asked one of the reps how I was regarded. "Some of them don't like you, Mary," she said, "but they respect you because you're fair." What the staff perceived as fair was really the consistency I installed in the department. That consistency was possible because I had decided what the rules were going to be, announced them to everyone, and then stuck by them. In return, I received trust and subsequently, respect.

- **Taking a stand saves time.** When you're clear and consistent about your principles, the people you work with are better able to anticipate what holds value for you. This is especially important when you're in a leadership position trying to establish a self-managing team. When team members are certain of your priorities and expected behavior, you can dedicate more of your time and effort to making progress, instead of rehashing old principles and guidelines.

- **Taking a stand positions you as someone who will take effective action for the sake of the company.** When you are known for being serious about your principles, you develop a "network of eyes" around the organization that will slip you valuable pieces of information that you can use to make a positive difference. That happened to me once when I was alerted of an obscene voice mail. Not only was this inappropriate, it was also a form of harassment, which added to my employee's already questionable performance. This resulted in me firing someone who'd started at the company the same time I did.

There are various degrees of termination at AOL, starting with a friendly agreement to part ways and ending with, "leave immediately and never come back." This guy was never to be allowed on the property ever again. Ever. Period.

But his association with AOL was important to his self-esteem, and he couldn't bear to completely let go. So, instead of reapplying, he got a job with an independent AOL content partner who had established an office in one of AOL's buildings. His new employer had no idea that he had this restriction, and AOL management had no idea that he was back until someone who knew him saw him. I was approached to take action, even though by that time, I had left the call center to work in human resources. We couldn't fire this offender because he wasn't working directly for AOL. But with a couple of well-placed phone calls, we could let our content partner know this guy was prohibited from AOL property. The issued was addressed and the problem was solved. Yet it wouldn't have happened if my informant didn't trust me to take action on behalf of the company.

- **Taking a stand sets you up for advancement.** Okay, so sometimes taking a stand at work is a "career limiting move" because the environment doesn't tolerate anything but the status quo. If so, it's likely you won't want to be there much longer anyway. But, if you're in a company where getting results and doing good business matters, taking a stand can set you up for getting recognized for your leadership and tenacity. The way I see it, few women have the nerve to speak up for themselves and their perspectives. Taking a stand is still considered a masculine tactic. As a result, men usually admire and respect it, especially those in executive ranks, you know, executive and *hiring* ranks.

Inside You Know Something's Not Right

Knowing when to take a stand isn't an exact science. Sometimes the best clue is your gut feeling. If something feels wrong, usually something *is* wrong; you just may not know exactly what it is. Don't doubt your instincts just because the evidence isn't immediately obvious. It will come, sooner if not later.

Even using the word *instincts* was a stretch to me in the early days. I used to be very careful about my female vocabulary. My education in a male-dominated engineering field combined with my "don't show any emotion if you want to gain respect as a woman" belief taught me to put such expressions as "I feel" on ice. I used language such as "I think" (and if I was daring, "I believe") that reflected more rational and logical realms - areas of thinking commonly associated with male thinking, although no gender really has a lock on so-called rational thinking.

In the early years, I actually felt embarrassed to bring my femaleness into the workplace. I thought the behavior code was "play like a man, act like a man." I didn't want to broadcast my femaleness at all. I usually wore jeans, chinos and other loose-fitting clothing to hide my female curves. I certainly didn't act in what I would have called a female way; giggly or silly. I didn't even like going to the bathroom with my purse. I thought it was some big signal, like a neon light over my head, "Period! Period! Period!"

I didn't care what women thought; I was worried about what men were thinking. The joke was, of course, on me. Men weren't thinking about me! But I was so caught up in neutralizing who I was that I was out of touch with the basic principle of being true to myself. As time went on, I discovered that my femaleness was my asset, a strength, not a cause for embarrassment. That's when I learned to trust my instincts, to claim the mysterious, immeasurable vocabulary of female feelings. I started using those feelings in my environment at work. Now they are my friends. Of course I may not react to them immediately, and I may not necessarily know what they mean right away either. But I discovered that noticing whether I was mad, sad, ready to cry or red with anger was important information that warranted my attention. (I also noticed men exhibited some behaviors that are effective. See what I mean by checking out the side bar *A Little Testosterone Goes A Long Way*.)

When your emotions are so strong you can't see the facts clearly, use trusted friends for feedback. Often friends can see things from an objective distance. They can hear you out, consider the details and tell you why you're feeling the way you are. Let them help you see reason before you act.

Side Bar
A Little a Testosterone Goes a Long Way

After being surrounded by mainly men in engineering school and the first seven years at AOL, I've had lots of opportunity to interact with and observe them. I've come to appreciate some of the ways men operate that serve them well in business. "What?!" I hear some of you saying." Yes, that's right – but read on. I'm not about to adopt all male behaviors. No way! I like my female attributes. And besides, I can't be a guy nearly well as a guy can; he has a "born-with-it" advantage. Still, a little testosterone goes a long way. Here are some male "testy" behaviors that bodacious women could benefit from stealing:

1. **Let negative words bounce off:** Men have a wonderful ability not to allow negative sticky notes to well...stick to them. "John, that report is missing a key conclusion!" "What do you mean you can't get it done by Friday, Frank? Don't you know how

important this account is?" These kinds of words seem to roll off men's backs. I say "seem" because I'm sure the words have some impact, but men don't let it show. They keep their cool. They don't emotionally absorb these words into their very beings like women often do, assuming that now they've been deemed unworthy and unlovable. Instead, men decide if the words have merit. If they do, they'll take action to solve the problem and move on.

2. **Say no without guilt:** Men don't seem nearly as concerned about making others happy as they are about taking care of their own needs. Sound selfish? It doesn't have to be. Consider that if men were so concerned about everyone else's needs they couldn't provide – financially, emotionally or otherwise – they'd disperse their efforts to the point that they'd be ineffective. So the only way to keep focused is to freely say no to anyone or anything that's not enabling you to achieve what's most important.

3. **Act as if you know what you're doing even if you're not quite sure:** I have to admit, I was alarmed and disturbed when I first noticed men at work doing this. "They are lying through their teeth!" I thought. Then I took a second look. These men were delivering on what they said they would. And they acted so confident that I assumed they knew exactly what they were doing. A male friend revealed to me that he didn't always know how he was going to accomplish a project, he just believed he'd figure it out. I finally realized it's a matter of believing in yourself and being resourceful. Lying had nothing to do with it.

4. **Feel free to talk about yourself and believe how wonderful you are:** Here I immediately think of a couple on their first date. The man wants to impress, so he tells the woman wonderful things about himself so she'll admire him. Sometimes he's successful, sometimes not, but he's willing to proudly show his colorful feathers. I admire that. That's risky; he might get rejected. But he knows he'll never get recognized if he doesn't try. The same is true in business.

5. **Don't read much past what's there:** Most women think men are a bit dull and simplistic not to notice all the hidden messages in Sue's tone or David's words. And compared to the typical female radar, they are! But, this also means men don't have to get caught up in all the energy draining sludge of what-ifs and hurt feelings. As women, we can't completely go against our natural wiring, but we can stop it from working against us. Differentiate between the facts of a situation and what else you intuitively picked up. Don't jump to conclusions about these ambiguous items, just keep them on the list of possibilities. Above all else, mentally move on to the next thing.

Don't Let This One Slide

It's up to you to decide at what point you're going to put your foot down. No one can tell you exactly how or when. But you'll know where that point is, even if it means facing the possible consequence of putting your relationship with your employer at risk. You'll know when you're feeling violated. You'll know when you're feeling used. You'll know when it's time to push back. It might be just a small moment, but it's the moment when you change forever.

Work-wise, for me, that time came about six months after I was passed over for the promotion I wanted and the position was filled by a man from the outside. He also became my new boss. Distracted by several projects, he left me alone at first, allowing me to do what I had already been doing for several years before he came on board. One day, I sent out an e-mail to a round of colleagues asking for their input on a project. My boss, of course, was on the list. I received some suggestions from others, but from my boss, I got an e-mail that felt like command and control. After six months of leaving me alone, suddenly he was in my e-mail box telling me what to do. I was just asking for input, but he was giving me orders. I knew a violation had happened, and I knew exactly what it was about.

The next morning we sat in my office for a previously scheduled meeting. I purposely jumped-started our conversation with, "You remember that e-mail you sent me last night? I've got to be honest, it sounded like you were telling me what to do. There's one thing I can't stand, and that's being told what to do."

If there was anyone in the world at that moment who had the right to tell me what to do, it was him. I accepted his positional power to do just that. But I also had years of autonomy, working with managers who recognized my ability to figure things out and take the initiative to get things done. So I added: "I've been in this role for several years now. And although you can tell me what to do and I will respect that, you should know that I will look for another situation to be in."

With a stunned look and defensive voice he responded, "But, I have my strong opinions!" To which I responded, "That's fine, I welcome strong opinions. I want to hear your point of view. I definitely believe that with lots of input, I can create a more effective result. But, in the end, *I'm* responsible for what happens." He conceded and agreed, "Well, okay."

From that moment, he respected my ability and my need to work without a heavy hand. I felt proud that I put a line in the sand. One benefit was that I got the behavior I wanted. But the longer lasting benefit was that I learned yet again that while risk comes with dangers of losing a job, it also comes with rewards. The risk of taking a stand is often rewarded with actually being able to keep the job you love.

Do a Little Planning, Then Just Do It!

You've tuned into your boundary channel, you've listened to your gut when it says something's not right, and you've decided it's time to take a stand. You want to stick up for yourself, perhaps at a whole new level. Okay, time to go for it. Time to just do it!

But wait, before you dive in, I suggest you do a little planning and thinking ahead. When you're not used to taking a stand, it's hard to think through everything in the moment. However, a little preparation goes a long way.

First and foremost: Determine what you're going to say and how you're going to say it. If you're saying something in person, write it out and say it out loud. Start with a statement of your main point, pause, and then add back-up information of what you mean and/or why you feel the way you do. No need to over explain. Practice in front of mirror, then on a trusted friend who can give you feedback. Get used to the wording so that it flows without having to look down at your paper. If you're writing an e-mail or letter, write it once, then put it aside and read it again later. Is it clear? Is it too long? Would the person know how you want them to respond? Again, ask a friend to put their eyes on it and get feedback.

Once you've determined what you're going to say and how you're going to say it, anticipate the response. If you're addressing one person, come up with at least two ways he or she may respond. How will you reply? If it's a small group, consider at least one response for each person.

Expect Some Push-Back

It's one thing to start a new job fresh with new relationships and new resolve to stand up for yourself, it's another to take your newfound stance into your current work environment. You are suddenly breaking the unspoken agreement that you will behave according to a certain code even when your principles are compromised. Suddenly, you're speaking up more, behaving more assertively.

Some people will embrace the change and be supportive. They enjoy seeing you be more gutsy! Others will feel as though you're drawing the line in *their* territory. Suddenly they can't move about so freely around you anymore. That's going to be uncomfortable for them, and that's when you can expect to get some push-back. You will certainly meet up with people who will test your resolve.

Being able to identify and counter resistance is the key to staying strong. One way to do this is to watch for the following six different characters that may emerge in reaction to your new backbone:

1. **The Caretaker:** Someone may decide to be your Caretaker and express such concerns as, "You haven't been yourself lately. Are you all right? You've been pretty edgy and people have been wondering if there is maybe something wrong at home." Of course you're edgy! You're practicing a new skill, and you're concerned that you might be doing it too forcefully, offending people unnecessarily when all you want to do is establish clear boundaries and standards for how you want to be treated. The Caretaker may be a true friend who is sincerely concerned with your welfare and

worried about your change in behavior or the Caretaker might be a false friend who is just gathering data to somehow leverage against you. Proceed with caution.

2. **The Gossip**: People may seem like friends by offering "helpful insights" into how you're being perceived and received by others. Such statements as, "People are saying you..." or "I heard so and so say you..." are never positive and encouraging. Beware of these tactics and keep your distance.

3. **The Distracter**: This person tries to get you off track from your main point by saying things that are seemingly valid. Statements may come in the form of criticizing your overall worthiness and emotional stability with comments such as, "Don't you think you're over-reacting or being just a little bit paranoid?" or "What you should really care about is…" Comments may also come in the form of planting seeds of doubt about your position. You might hear, "Are you sure?", "Did you do sufficient research?" or "According to my years of experience (conversations, insider information, etc.), what's really happening is…." These kinds of questions and comments are designed to escalate tension and rattle you. Stay calm, stay focused on your message. Carefully choose which to answer. If you feel yourself getting rattled, shut down the rest of the conversation and go back to your main point. Don't let anyone get the upper hand.

4. **The Fidgeter**: Another person who engages in rattling maneuvers. You're tense. You're uncertain. You're trying to express your concerns clearly and unemotionally. But the person you're talking to keeps looking at his or her watch, shuffling and reorganizing papers and glancing out the door. They're uncomfortable. All this fidgeting activity is making you feel rushed and unheard. Stand

your ground. Stay focused and take your time.
They'll just have to wait until you're finished.

5. **The Superior**: This person is someone whom you've
confided in before, someone whose opinion you trust,
like a boss or a mentor whose guidance you have
sought out in the past. This is usually a one-down
relationship, with you in the down position. It's not
uncommon to outgrow your mentors and advisors.
In fact, you're expected to. But many superiors feel
insecure when they see you assert independence, so
you may hear expressions such as, "Awe, come on,
you don't really mean that" or "You sure aren't the
sweet woman I thought I knew." Or they will refer
back to a privileged piece of information you shared
with them in the early days and use it to remind you
that you came from "humble beginnings". This is
done to invite you to return to your less bodacious
ways.

6. **The Threatener**: This person threatens consequences
that are out of proportion to merely speaking your
mind: "If you ever say that again, you will be sorry."
It's hard enough to gather the courage to speak your
mind and take a stand when your expectations are
reasonable. When someone overreacts to your
message in a threatening way, try not to take the
warnings personally, but do take note. Write down
what was said, word for word. You never know when
you'll need that information.

Remember these characters when you start feeling tension
escalating. Remind yourself that this is just a strategy. Temporarily
detach from your emotions, perhaps by pretending you're hovering
near the ceiling looking down as if watching a play. Tell the person
you've stood your ground with that you believe you have expressed

your position as clearly as possible, and end the discussion. Don't try to look for satisfaction when the person you're talking to is behaving in any of the ways I've just mentioned. It's a good idea to follow-up with a memo or e-mail outlining your points one final time. Writing it out is not to drive your points into the ground. It documents your expectations in a clear-headed, unemotional way, and it creates an official record that you've expressed your expectations in unambiguous terms. Save or print a copy of your memo or e-mail for future reference.

Side Bar

Take Charge of Your Financial Future

There is one enduring lesson we can all take from the New Economy: We're responsible for our careers and our financial security. It's not too late to get started. But it's not too soon either. Here are a few things I learned:

- **Assume you will have to do more than earn a salary, save, and draw Social Security:** Simple passbooks savings, combined with Social Security will not help you build a nest-egg for a comfortable, secure retirement. Your financial future depends on you taking an active role in managing your money today.

- **Start investing now:** Use your money to make money. That's one secret of wealthy people all over the world. There are many investment choices: 401K account, IRA accounts, pension funds, mutual funds, stocks, bonds, certificate of deposit, money market accounts, saving accounts, gold or precious metals, real estate, and more. Assess your risk tolerance and only get involved in investment options that allow you to sleep at night.

- **Get expert help:** Book, magazines, and Web sites are available to give you basic principles and ideas for making early retirement a reality. These resources are a great way to get oriented, but the vocabulary alone can be overwhelming! Hiring a professional who has dedicated their career to understanding financial management just makes sense. We do it when we need medial or legal help, why not financial? Good financial planners will more than pay for themselves. They'll help you understand your dreams in financial terms and help you design a plan to reach those dreams. Select your financial planner carefully. Get recommendations from friends and family. Interview several by phone or in person. Only choose someone you're comfortable with, and remember, you can switch to someone else at any time.

- **Learn how the stock market works:** For some, the very thought of learning about the stock market makes them want to forget the whole idea of retiring. "I'll just work all my life until I die, rather than get that pit in my stomach like I did when struggling with fifth grade word problems." But, it's not as daunting as it seems. Really. Buy an easy-to-read book on investing in stocks, how analysts evaluate them and how to understand typical stock market behavior. Watch financial news programs to gain confidence and further your knowledge.

- **Keep it simple:** You can always get more sophisticated as you gain experience and if you want to be more daring. The more you're involved and understand what's really happening with your money the more confident you'll be.

Don't Call Me That!

The hardest part about taking a stand for what you believe in is the worry that people may stop liking you. (Some may admire you and love it!) By putting a stake in the ground, you are essentially telling your associates that how they've been treating you won't work anymore. If you effectively get them to change, you will win. And by winning, you will have beaten them. It takes a lot of bodaciousness to be comfortable with the notion of competition, especially when the one who loses out is someone you work with. In her book, *The Princessa, Machiavelli for Women*, Harriet Rubin writes:

> "Most women cannot win. Not because a woman cannot fight strategically. But because no one wants her to win, and often neither does she. Both she and her opponents see to it that she fails. She herself may become consumed with guilt if she wins – guilt for having created another's loss. Men hate losing to a woman; this can prompt a counterattack. And to another woman, a triumphant woman is a lifelong threat."

To good girls and Bodacious Women alike, it's not pleasant to be perceived as threatening, not nice at all. We're socially encoded to be accommodating, to be havens of comfort and security. If our agenda means putting someone out, we often choose ourselves.

When my call center associate told me that a few of the reps didn't like me, I imagined that I might have been called the b-word now and then. When you think about it, the very behaviors which make women successful in the corporate world cause us to be labeled "bitch". What helped me is not giving naysayers much weight. The internal satisfaction of taking care of myself meant far more to me than the opinion of someone who didn't want to understand.

Part of growing and expanding your bodacious boundaries entails pushing back on someone else's territory. You could do it as nicely and as well-intentioned as possible, but if your ambition conflicts with someone else's (which is bound to happen now and then), you can count on having those words uttered about you. Most achievement-oriented women have, so don't worry, you'll be in good company!

When Someone Takes a Stand With You

As difficult as it is to be on the giving end, it's also uncomfortable being on the receiving end of someone taking a stand with you. You've got to keep yourself emotionally balanced. You can't control the vehemence of someone's feelings, but you can influence the atmosphere of the confrontation or conflict. Make people feel they are safe to express what they need to, that what they say won't come back to haunt them, and that you sincerely care about their well-being. Here are some tips I learned from my years at AOL:

- **If the conflict happens in a public setting, quietly suggest you move to a private area such as your office or conference room.** Close the door and give the person your complete attention. So much of the aftermath of any confrontation is feeling embarrassed for getting emotional in front of others. The person who is upset with you may later be grateful for your consideration, even if he or she doesn't show it right then and there.

- **Give the person the floor.** Try not to interrupt while the person is speaking, even if you're tempted to correct a detail. Let him or her vent. Only stop the conversation if it gets personal or loses focus.

- **Don't allow outside interruptions.** Don't answer your phone. Tell anyone who might knock on your door that you will talk to them later. This moment – as well as your attention – is reserved for the person in your office.

- **Seek to understand the person's perspective.** This doesn't mean you must agree with him or her. But you must at least try to see from their point of view. If you really can't "get it" or if the conversation gets more and more confusing, tell the person that you want to understand and that you need some time to think over what has been said. Offer to schedule another appointment in a day or two to regroup and talk things over again. By that time, the conversation won't be so emotionally charged; the person will have felt heard. Then you might be able to come to a clearer understanding.

- **Know exactly what will satisfy the complainer.** Does this person need an apology from you or someone else? Are they requesting a change of behavior on your part or a specific action? If you can honestly give what he or she wants, do it. If you can't, explain why in a clear, concise manner. Know that by listening, you've at least given the person something valuable and significant – respect.

- **Apologize sincerely and without "buts".** If you're sorry, say so without trying to wriggle off any hooks of responsibility. To hear, "Look, I'm really sorry, but...." is very unsatisfactory for the person, and unbodacious for you. If you deserve to take responsibility, take responsibility, even if it means taking it on the chin. You will cultivate more respect and loyalty in the long run.

Culture Shock

Taking a stand is one of the most bodacious actions you can take. By simply saying, "This is what I believe and want," you are creating a culture shift in your life that will ripple beyond your immediate goals in any area.

You will be turning on a mechanism within your own spirit that will continue to assist you to take a stand. With time and practice, this will become easier.

You will be changing your immediate environment from one of neglect or disrespect to one of respect, achievement, pride, and an enduring sense of self-worth that will prevail no matter the circumstance.

By setting effective boundaries, you will be impacting your friends and associates in a new way. Some people will be inspired by your example, others will simply retreat from your life. Nevertheless, you will be attracting more powerful, self-actualized, and bodacious relationships.

Your conversations will change. You won't be focusing as much on problems, complaints, and difficult situations. You will be talking about innovations, ambition, possibilities, ideas, and ideals.

This is a time of shift and change. It's a time to use the Now Economy as a portal to step into a bigger, bolder, and more authentic you. To do this, the Bodacious Woman surrounds herself with friends, family, and co-workers who support her vision, respect her boundaries, and have the courage and sense of adventure to take their own journey of bodacious self-discovery.

To Build Your Bodacious Career...

- Be clear about your emotional, psychological and physical boundaries. Write them down.

- Pay attention to how others treat you. Don't let negative treatment go unchecked.

- Take a stand for yourself when needed. Plan what you will say, how you say it, and anticipate responses. Be aware of the six characters that might show up to push back.

- Remember that your self-respect is far more valuable than undeservedly being called a bitch.

- Be respectful of others when they take a stand with you. Imagine what actions and behaviors you'd do to demonstrate respect.

Thrive on Shift and Change

In Building Your Bodacious Career...

- Does continual change excite or drain you?

- Are you waiting to have all the knowledge and information you need to confidently make decisions?

- Do you have a proactive strategy for managing change in your career and life?

Welcome to the Wilderness

You might as well enjoy it, because you're going to be here for awhile. The key is to accept the fact that life in the Now Economy will be confusing, surprising and unfamiliar. Will you worry and obsess about things that can go wrong or will you find new vistas thrilling, knowing full well there will be hazards along the way? You can be certain there will also be rewards for bodaciously venturing forth!

There's a reason why this chapter title includes *shift* along with *change*. I'm hoping to encourage you to focus just as much on the uncertainty of shifting times as on positive end results. It seems to be human nature to focus on the end result, but it's in the process where the good stuff happens; growth, self-discovery, humor, amazement, creativity. It takes a lot of nerve and spirit to actually thrive during the shift stage. That's where you'll find many Bodacious Women, which is a good thing, because in the Now Economy, I haven't seen very many processes culminating into any definitive finalities. Change is continuous. Having a good time yet? Maybe not yet. For you, the shift stage could be full of pain and fear. Maybe you're worried you won't be able to keep up with the ongoing education that's necessary just to stay current with your profession. Maybe a marriage is suffering. Maybe you're afraid that the next layoff will include you. Maybe you're afraid that after shifting, your loved ones won't like who you've become. Or worse, maybe you won't like who you've become.

This is what William Bridges, author of *Transitions* and *Managing Transitions*, calls the "emotional wilderness". It's fear associated with knowing you're inextricably along for the Now Economy ride, without any clear idea of the final outcome, and very concerned that you may lose something precious along the way. These are very natural concerns. Yet the bodacious way gives you the guidance and inspiration you need to actively design and achieve the high-performance life you're capable of. It's up to you to keep designing and then redesigning the next versions of how you want to be: Bodacious Career 2.0; Bodacious Career 3.0, and so on.

Let me forewarn you: Shifting may cause you to go through some major culture shocks and climate changes. As with every alteration in your life you create or any alteration that comes you way (let's face it, some events are out of your hands), you may feel alien to your new circumstances. Don't worry, you'll grow into them.

Change is Inevitable; Growth is Optional

At AOL, my entire career was about rapid shift and change. For the first seven years, I was totally focused on the call center. I was promoted from customer service rep to trainer to training manager and then to call center manager. Though we were always shifting and changing to serve customers, the scene had some familiarities. I knew the staff, I knew the rhythms of the day, and I knew the soundtrack of hundreds of voices answering thousands of calls every day: "Thank you for calling America Online. My name is – How may I help you?"

Soon other areas of my life – namely one last-ditch effort to save my marriage after a year's separation – demanded that I make another major change. With the hours being a call center manager demanded, I worried that I wasn't giving my husband the time and attention he needed to feel that I was recommitted to our relationship. I needed to shift some of the energy I was dedicating to AOL into reviving my marriage. AOL needed a fully dedicated call center manager to run the growth we were still experiencing. I knew this move would negatively impact my work and I didn't want to mar my performance record.

I considered leaving AOL altogether. But that seemed too drastic. I loved the company, and it was one place in my life where I could count on feeling safe, confident and competent. I was respected, and I was earning every bit of that respect. Despite its high-pressure environment, AOL was a place where I could relax and be my best self. I didn't want to give that up.

So I started looking around the company to see where else I might be able to offer value. I thought about the increasing belief that managers would have a huge impact on how well we were going to grow. I knew I could help the company in developing and influencing this group of contributors. It was amazing to realize that after 10 years and more than 1200 employees, the company still had no management training program. We were all so busy getting day-to-day work done that we were neglecting the ongoing professional development needs of the very people who were pivotal in getting results.

Setting my sites on switching over to corporate human resources, I thought I could have a greater impact throughout the organization and maybe remove myself from the pressure-cooker atmosphere of the call center. Instead of ten- to twelve-hour days, maybe I could reduce it to eight or nine and get home to my husband at a decent time.

I didn't wait until I saw a job posting. I took the initiative and contacted the new vice-president of human resources. He and I knew each other slightly because of a few call center employee issues I addressed with him. To him, I was a line manager who happened to have five years of training experience already under her belt plus an extensive history with the company. I thought since he was commissioned with developing a full-fledged HR group, maybe he could use someone with my background and understanding of how the company really worked. Additionally, he respected the fact that I was really into the purpose of building the company through people.

Although I was motivated to make a change for personal reasons, I emphasized to him my desire to help build the company from the inside out by quickly developing skilled managers. I didn't want him to know about my personal life, partly because it wasn't his concern but also because I felt like it was the part of my life where I was failing. I was concerned my reputation for being competent, efficient, and successful, remain intact. I didn't want anyone to doubt my abilities. So, courage in hand, I asked for a new role, one I hoped would continue to further my success.

He made me a job offer; corporate training manager. My burgeoning Bodacious Career life took another turn.

The Art and Science of Making Those Dang Decisions

A world of constant change requires us to make so many dang decisions! Effective decision making is a strategic skill for a Bodacious Career and life. Forging a career in the Old Economy was mainly about what you could produce, usually in an environment that was fairly consistent and stable. Education and hard work was the focus. Forging a career in today's Now Economy is more about being able to effectively apply all of your education, knowledge, and experiences to a never-ending cycle of change. Knowledge, analysis, and good decision making are now the keys to success.

Deciding what you want for lunch or who to call when your computer acts up, these are no-brainer type decisions. But it's easy to get overwhelmed with more complex decisions to the extent that you want to cover your eyes and just pick something out of a hat. What part of the company's new product will you eliminate in order to make the launch deadline? Which internal customer's expectation will be compromised because of budget cuts? Should you look for another job or hang in there?

I may have never become an engineer, but one thing engineering school taught me was how to break down a problem and figure out the best solution. Using the engineering method of solving a problem makes thinking through a decision a little less daunting. Early in my AOL career, I was amazed how much I used this handy little skill. You certainly don't have to be an engineer to understand this approach (there's no math involved if that's your worry). And, even though engineering seems like a science, at some point, it becomes an art form just like everything else. Here's how it works:

1. **Define the problem or situation.** This can often be the toughest part because often you think you know but maybe it's not clear. Can you express the problem in a single question? If others are involved, do they agree

this is the question to be answered? Is there a truer question underneath the assumed one? Be specific and very clear about what you're really trying to figure out. It does you (and others) no good to solve the wrong problem.

2. **Determine what you already know.** What do you already know about the situation? Write out the facts of the situation surrounding the decision, not opinions or feelings but objective data. For example, name the new company product and list all of its existing features. Note how this produce fits into the company's strategy and contribution. Make a list of every internal and external person or constituency the product effects. Rate each feature in terms of importance by constituency. What do you need to know? Go find it; be it from a report, from a web search or tapping into someone's knowledge (here's where those relationships you've been building for your Bodacious Career that we talked about in Chapter Two come into play again).

3. **List your options.** What are your options? Brainstorm a list of all possible ways to deal with your well-defined problem. Now rank these options from most preferred to least preferred. What's your best educated guess on the impact of each option? If needed do some research to gain further understanding. Which option(s) are most likely to happen and why?

4. **Choose the best option for you.** Given this expanded understanding of the situation's landscape, what's the best choice for you? Often this becomes clear as you list all the options. If not, look carefully at how you ranked the options and the related impact. Keep in mind that complex decisions always come with

trade-offs. What is your gut telling you? Which ones can you live with?

5. **Go for it!** Given the time pressures most of us have, it's tempting to jump to this step and make some kind of decision just to get it over with. I've found that taking even a short amount of time to analyze and reflect on a problem brings huge benefits and can avoid negative consequences. Still, after you've made a decision, it's time to go for it! Stick to your decision. Consider how you're going to implement it. Then go!

6. **If needed, fail fast, learn and move on:** No matter how hard you try, some decisions don't turn out to be the best ones. When that happens, quickly re-group and re-choose. Take the stake out and replant it. Sometimes a change in customer need or other unforeseeable factor causes a completely different decision and direction. Sometimes only an adjustmentis required. In any case, fail fast, learn and move on.

Launch the Change Reaction

Talk about culture shock! You know that feeling when you dive into deep water and there's an invisible but unmistakable line where you pass from warmth into significantly cooler water? In one instant, I passed through one level where I was managing an operation of 250 people, seven days a week, and servicing hundreds of thousands of customers to being what *Fast Company* magazine calls a "Unit of One". In my former life, I was surrounded by the buzz, the call center energy, people always walking past my door. The day I packed up my things and moved to the building next door, I went from that buzz to a stifling silence. I remember going down a carpeted hallway, carrying my box of belongings and passing office after office after office after office. And I could hear nothing. It was so quiet! Where was everybody?!

I thought I was on the track to gearing down, having children, becoming a stay-at-home mom, and being a wife in a functional, if not joyful, marriage. We even bought a five-bedroom house in the suburbs. In time, I'd have a minivan to go with it. But for now, my main task was to settle into this new role and create training that would help develop managers, and fast!

During my stint as corporate training manager from 1995 to 1999, AOL mushroomed from 1200 employees to 12,000. Revenues went from $100 million to $2 billion. We went from a small, domestic company sharing an office building to a multinational organization with over 12 major locations throughout the world. A ton of things were changing!

We could have been swamped by panic or chaos. We could have focused on the wrong objectives, choosing to put out brightly burning fires that were ultimately inconsequential instead of focusing on the larger mission. This was the height of what I call AOL adrenaline. It was exciting. It was explosive. And we consistently knew what we were about, what we valued, and what our ultimate goal was.

I quickly learned how to implement change. Here are some ideas I found worked well. Consider these when launching your own Bodacious Career change.

EXPECT SOME INITIAL DISCOMFORT

Not only did I experience environmental culture shock all alone in my quiet training office, but I had to create my new job from scratch. Fortunately, nearly all of my previous positions required some level of invention. Still, I'd never built a training program for an entire company. My ability to perform would be seen by literally everyone in the company, a company that was constantly growing.

Shift and change. Remember, it comes with the territory. And this is where the emotional wilderness that William Bridges talks about in *Managing Transitions* is especially evident. As Bridges writes, "[Planners and implementers] forget that while the first task of change management is to understand the destination and how to get there, the first task of transition management is to convince people to leave home." Your own personal transition management challenge is to convince yourself to leave home, whether "home" is a department at work, old personal habits or a home life that has become toxic.

You will feel uncomfortable for a time. Old weaknesses and insecurities that you managed to efficiently camouflage in the old systems suddenly make themselves obvious again. You might even get sick. The stress of change can lower your immunity system and cause you to catch the flu, a cold or a case of hives. You may temporarily feel like a mess.

LEAD WITH YOUR VALUE

Trust that you can be resourceful. As you research options, look beneath the surface. The alchemy of your passions, combined with external needs may create an opportunity for you that hadn't existed before. When I started looking around AOL for alternatives to my 10 to 12-hour days in the call center, I didn't know the human resource vice-president was considering including a corporate training manager on his team. I just believed I could make a difference and had what it took to do it. The vice-president saw that. He recognized my package of skills, dedication and experiences, and knew he could leverage them in a way that would benefit the entire company, not just the call center. So he asked me to go corporate.

CREATE CHANGE IN HALF-STEPS

At AOL, we were creating change in giant strides, but in my personal life, I discovered the best way to change was in manageable half-steps. Half-steps help you test whether the change process is giving you desired results. When we lose weight gradually, we stand a better chance of keeping it off. When we give ourselves half-step goals aimed towards a huge revolution in our lives, we can stop, acknowledge our progress, congratulate ourselves for any improvement, and then step up to the next level.

I could have decided to leave AOL entirely in favor of saving a marriage that ultimately would not have been saved anyway. And I considered it. But that giant stride would have been in conflict with my personal commitment to be part of this exciting adventure of building a company that would truly change the way the world communicates. The half-step of finding another position within the company allowed me to still be part of this adventure while reserving my time and energy to nurture my marriage.

GET OUTSIDE PERSPECTIVE WHENEVER YOU CAN

You may not know how good you really are until you leave your fishbowl. When we're sealed up in our own environment, working hard and focusing on the tasks immediately in front of us, we can lose perspective. It's easy to fall in the trap of self-criticism without any real sense of how we compare to external colleagues. I say get out there! You may discover that you are further ahead than you thought.

That came home to me loud and clear the first year I was invited to make a presentation at the Ken Blanchard Companies' annual client conference. This is a high-profile event, in which Blanchard's preferred clients gather, compare their experiences and results, and learn from one another.

I wanted to do something that would blow their socks off, something that was really motivating, fun, energetic, useful, and would show off our training. I assembled some rock music, a MTV-like company video, and a killer PowerPoint presentation that told the story of our hyper-growth and how Blanchard helped us through the adventure. This was one bodacious program, I thought.

When it was show time, my hands were clammy, my heart was pounding. The room was packed, the lights dimmed. It was on with the show! The response was amazing. Wide eyes, lots of smiles and applause greeted me. Marjorie Blanchard, Ken's wife shot up and gave me a big hug when it was all over. I found out later that my presentation scored the highest that year.

At that moment, I began to realize how bodacious my AOL career was and what a powerful position I had carved out for myself. At that moment, I started to realize my growing dissatisfaction with not getting the full credit I felt I deserved. I wouldn't have appreciated that fact if I was back in Northern Virginia focusing on the next training rollout.

A few days later, at the conference's closing dinner, I received an unexpected award. As Ken congratulated me, he asked, "So, when are you going to come work with us?" Here I was, in front of 200 clapping people, getting a job offer from one of the country's most highly respected business leaders. Then, a few weeks after I returned home, I got a voice mail. "Hi Mary. A colleague of mine saw you at the Blanchard client conference. I'm with a company looking for an organizational development director and wanted to know if you're available." Talk about getting perspective!

Organizational development director – precisely the position at AOL that I lost because I for not being strategic enough! Still, I took a pass on both opportunities. Life sure has a way of being ironic. My personal strategy was about to take a different direction; grad school.

MAKE CHANGE FUN

Steve Case was a master at keeping up the spirits of AOL employees. No occasion was too small for a party. In the earliest, cash-strapped days, we celebrated with beer bashes on Friday afternoons. Steve believed in fostering a spirit of community among employees and he often shared milestones at all-hands meetings which were followed by increasingly lavish parties. I remember one party in particular where Steve bit off more than he could chew.

It was March 1995, and we were celebrating the two million member mark. By this time, AOL parties had gone big time and the company wisely held its parties off-site with rented buses to keep revelers away from their car keys. And, wow, could we revel!

Steve was strutting around wearing a fantastic black leather bomber jacket with a gold AOL logo embroidered on the back. People kept coming up to him saying how much they loved it. Either he'd had one compliment too many or one beer too many, because at the height of the party, he went up to a microphone and announced, "Since everyone likes my jacket so much, here's a challenge for you: If we reach five million members by next year this time, every one will get a jacket of their own!"

The room exploded with cheers. Everyone loved the challenge. We rededicated our focus to increasing the membership from two million to five million in just 12 months. Amazingly, we did it! And Steve came up with the goods; we all got spiffy leather jackets.

Shared fun is as much a galvanizing force as shared work. There's a lot of leverage that can be made from memories of laughter and good times. Steve was certainly the hero for making such a bodacious offer and delivering on his promise.

TAKE A STEP OVER WHEN IT'S STRATEGIC

In the Now Economy, you're no longer limited to the two-dimensional career ladder. You can move all around the landscape – up, down, sideways, way over there, way over here, over to a different industry - if it's a strategically bodacious move. You can even move down in order to shoot back up to a higher level. This is not a loss of stature, this is a bodacious shift in position. But it only makes sense if you're doing it strategically. In AOL's earliest days, Steve Case took a step down from head honcho to vice-honcho because the company was about to go public. Senior leadership agreed that institutional investors probably wouldn't have faith in a company led by someone so young. So Steve took a demotion in order to position the company's leadership as being experienced and investment worthy. Once AOL's Wall Street objectives were met and the company proved its performance potential to investors, young Steve Case resumed his title and role.

LEVERAGE YOUR CHOICES

There will be changes and choices in your life where half-steps may not apply. These are sometimes sudden, life-changing decisions. When those opportunities come along, make the most self-affirming choice you can, and then give it all you've got.

As I've said before, messages can come in stereo. For me, one channel of change always seems to be in support of the other, if only to give me the confidence and sense of self to make the tough decisions. The first choice was to end my marriage. In this second round, I had invested almost two and a half years of honest and earnest effort into the reconciliation of this unhealthy relationship. My worried parents had watched as I walked back into a marriage that offered only pain and emotional damage. I knew I had given it my best shot and was ready to let it go.

But this wasn't going to be the frightened escape I'd made a couple of years earlier. This time, I would coolly make the arrangements I needed to leave the marriage safely. One morning after my husband left for work, I loaded my car with clothes and a few personal belongings. When he came home, we headed to the counselor's office for our appointment. I'd made arrangements for a friend to meet me there afterward. I also had already lined up a place to stay for a few nights until I found something more permanent. I was positioned for flight, but knew I needed all my strength to put my flight plan into action.

During our session, I broke the news to my husband. As he sat stunned in the chair next to me, I suddenly felt all the years of emotional exhaustion culminating into that one moment in time. A nauseating rush cascaded over my body. I stood up, steadying myself as I made for the door, then opened it, and walked through to a new way of life.

A few months later, I was ready to decide about my career. I'd already asked my boss why I wasn't fully recognized for my abilities. But that was a dead-end road. He'd chosen to fill a position with someone else. I wanted to do the same kind of work of building the people side of organizations. I also wanted more challenge. And if I couldn't find that at AOL, I already knew other organizations would be more than happy to have me. Even though I could jump right into a new position at another company, I wanted to learn more about the organizational development field first. I decided the next step was grad school.

But which grad school, where, and when? I knew a few people with such degrees, so I started asking them. I checked out Web sites and called program offices for information. Another task was deciding what I preferred as a school experience. Did I want something local? Was I after a more theoretical slant or an application perspective? What was the cost? I also needed to investigate prerequisite and application requirements. Did I have to take any kind of entrance exam? Write a paper? Get recommendations? Have a faculty interview? When was the deadline?

I narrowed my choices to two schools, both required the Graduate Entrance Exam (GRE). So I set out to find what was involved. I discovered that to make my application deadlines, I'd had to take the exam in about two weeks! So, I signed up and crammed until test day. I postponed the rest of my life while preparing for that exam, taking practice tests again and again.

My results were okay, but nothing that screamed genius. Fortunately, the applications gave me other opportunities to persuade the schools to accept me, like including letters of recommendation.

Here's where I got bodacious. The schools wanted two letters; I gave them four! And I pulled out the big guns. I asked Ken Blanchard and Steve Case to sign letters endorsing my abilities, which they did. I remember getting an e-mail from Steve's assistant telling me the letter was ready. I rushed upstairs to pick it up. Steve was in his office. With letter in hand, I nervously knocked on his door and peeked in to thank him. He looked up and smiled. "Thanks for the letter, Steve." I blurted. "This is really going to put my average GRE scores over the top!" He laughed and wished me the best of luck, and I walked away with gold in my hand.

But the most difficult challenge was posed by my first school of choice – Pepperdine University in California. Their application package included an extremely lengthy questionnaire that probed into my emotional life, stability, and self-knowledge. I can understand their concern. Accepting a student is an investment for them too. This could have been a showstopper. Forget the GREs, forget the to-die-for letters of recommendation. I was in the middle of one of life's major crises; a separation leading to divorce. They may decide to pass me up with the reasoning that I needed more time to heal before taking on the demanding load of their curriculum. I decided to play it as honestly, straightforwardly, and proactively as I knew how. I told them where I was in the divorce process, about the support I was receiving from my family and friends, and of my confidence that I would be a successful student.

On May 4, 1998, I came home to my apartment to find an envelope with Pepperdine's return address. Inside the letter read: "Dear Mary: On behalf of the faculty and staff of Pepperdine University George L. Graziadio School of Business and Management, please accept our congratulations on your acceptance into the Masters of Science in Organizational Development (MSOD) Program."

I was in!

But there was still one more change yet to come.

The Choice is Always Yours

Remember that fateful day when I forgot my pants at work? That wasn't long after I'd received my acceptance letter. It suddenly became very clear to me that I was mentally and emotionally over-extended. I needed to make a change to take better care of myself, especially if I was going to have enough time and energy for grad school.

Part of me wasn't ready to leave AOL as I was still finalizing my divorce, and the thought of starting a whole new job while starting grad school didn't make much sense either. Still, something had to give, so I asked my boss about working part-time. Part-time. That's an oxymoron at a fast-paced, highly demanding company like AOL. I went for it anyway. AOL didn't want me to leave, so they created a training instructor position for me that required giving up my manager role. I chose to take a step down to get the space I needed. Over the next few months, I tried to make the arrangement work, but even the partial load was almost 40 hours a week and still too much. The time had come to depart this company I loved so much. I walked into my boss's office and gave him the news that I wanted to reduce my hours yet again, this time to zero.

"Oh, you'll be back in six months," he said. No, I thought. This time it was "goodbye."

The decision was made. And I wasn't going to unmake it. It was time to see what the big, wide world had in store for me. It was hard to imagine a career outside of AOL, but at 33, it wasn't too late for me to discover it. Grad school felt like the right transition to make.

Before I ended my Bodacious AOL Career, I understood at least one thing on a political and personal level; ending well was vitally important for me and my relationships. It doesn't do you or others much good to take 10 years of your life and make your last official interaction full of resentment. Nothing had to be perfect to see all the amazing, positive experiences AOL had given me. I knew that my last days at AOL would be what I made them, so I purposely decided to bring closure my way. Even though I didn't ask for the circumstances that led to my divorce and leaving AOL, the choice to end those relationships were mine.

I chose my last day to be the day after I finished a series of workshops for a vice-presidents group I admired. Instead of each workshop feeling like a hassle, it felt like my last personal imprint on the organization that had given me so much. As my last week started, I made a list of people I wanted to say goodbye to. I made a point of seeing many of them before I left, but soon my last day would come and I still hadn't seen them all. I knew the power of e-mail we shared with the world would be the most effective and appropriate solution to saying goodbye to those I didn't see in person.

Sitting down to write my goodbye e-mail took me back to my senior year high school yearbook. My friends scribed "Love you forever!" all over its pages. We were so serious and clueless! But it meant something then, and what I was about to compose meant something now. I wanted to use all I had learned and experienced to say something important and lasting. I stared at my monitor while my brain poured over fond memories and my heart rode the emotional waves.

Then I knew. Of all the things I could say about all the amazing things we'd done, I felt the most authentic and meaningful was to focus on my experience with people. Steve Case often talked about how the human experience was really at the core of the online experience. I typed my last e-mail as an AOL employee, stood up, switched off my computer, slid my chair toward the desk, picked my briefcase up off the floor, turned in my badge, and went home.

I sold the minivan and replaced it with a Porsche. That's the car I would later drive west to California, with my mother riding shotgun.

FROM: Mary Foley
DATE: 01/29/99
SUBJECT: Thank you!

Studies show that people don't usually stay long term at a company because of the money, power or prestige. Nope, it's usually because they can work on challenging stuff, and do that with some great people. That's the case with me.

All of you have, in some way, contributed to my experience of working with great people. Each of you has given me something, be it a sincere smile, an encouraging word, your belief in me or your sage advice and helpful feedback. Some of you have been role models and mentors. For that I want to say THANK YOU!

I wish you all the best of everything in your continued adventure with AOL. I'm sure there are more great things to come! If you'd like to stay in touch, I'll only be an e-mail away...on the "other side."

To Build Your Bodacious Career...

• Be honest with yourself about how you handle change in your career and life. Make a commitment to do what you can to thrive, not just survive, in today's constantly shifting environment.

• Add some analysis to your decision making, then do a gut check. Identify at least one decision you must make and apply Mary's engineering approach.

• Strategically manage the change in your career and life. Consider one or more approaches outlined in this chapter or create your own.

Bonus Insert:

From Layoffs to Relighting Your Bodacious Career: Basics for Navigating Job Change

Shift and change in the Now Economy often involves changing jobs and companies. Here are some basics for dealing with layoffs to restarting your Bodacious Career.

How to Survive a Layoff

Layoffs are a fact of life in the Now Economy. It's a terrible moment to hear that, through no fault of your own, your company has decided to let you go. It's equally no fun to be a "survivor" of a round of cuts, to then come to work the next day and find yourself surrounded by empty desks that once belonged to people you worked and laughed with. No matter whether you are victim or survivor of a layoff, it may feel like the end of a dream. But it doesn't have to be the end of hope. You can leverage the experience and come out the better for it.

IF YOU GET LAID OFF

- **Don't take it personally:** You don't need self-recrimination to make you feel worse than you already do. Many layoffs happen because of a company's financial situation. It's not about you, it's about the company's survival. In addition, companies often use the layoff process as a way of getting rid of "dead wood", that doesn't necessarily mean you were fired for lack of performance. If you can look back at your time with the company and know you performed well, take comfort in that.

- **Don't sign anything right away:** In the meeting where you get the bad news, they may shove a stack of documents for you to digest right away and sign. Don't. Take at least 24 hours and consider showing the documents to an attorney to make sure you understand the details. You can be sure your employer did. Many agreements are written in favor of the employer.

- **Negotiate for more:** It's possible you will be able to negotiate a more beneficial severance package, such as one to two weeks of pay for each year you have worked at the company, the ability to continue to use your office and phone (or voice mail) as you transition, and reference letters from top management. Expect that if you don't ask, they won't offer.

- **Explore a consulting option with the company:** Your position may be eliminated but that doesn't necessarily mean the workload is. If you can redefine your job in terms of smaller projects, you may be able to renegotiate a consulting relationship with the company. You stand to save the company money and keep a steady cash flow while you consider other options. Consulting also keeps you on good terms with the company, which may benefit you once the company starts to staff up again.

- **Use company-sponsored outplacement services:** Almost every major company layoff includes helping former employees transition to the next job by providing professional outplacement services. You can get expert advice on exploring your aptitude, talents and passions; learning interviewing techniques, and finding leads for jobs at other companies. This is a very valuable service, so use it!

- **Start attending meetings of your professional association and other business gatherings:** Get out of the house as much as you can; meet new people, explore all options and possibilities. Even consider working as a temp. Temp agencies fill openings from basic clerical work to CEO positions. This is a great way to expand your network of contacts, learn new skills, earn money, and keep your confidence intact.

- **Throw "Pink Slip" Parties:** Instead of slinking off in shame or embarrassment, use a company layoff as the excuse for a party to bring together your fellow employees in an upbeat, low-pressure, social environment. Invite the best recruiters in your area. Help yourself and others while you're at it.

- **Stay in touch with former coworkers:** Many survivors may feel badly after you've left and want to know you're okay. It can feel awkward for both parties to contact each other after a layoff. But a simple phone call or e-mail is all it takes to melt the discomfort. What's more important is keeping your network of Bodacious Career relationships intact. So identify a handful of people to stay in touch with, and always make the first move.

IF YOU KEEP YOUR JOB

- **Connect your position with corporate goals:** Know exactly how your job helps your company meet its current operational and profit objectives. Be able to talk about your function in terms of business strategy. Know how the company is doing in its market, among customers, and on the stock exchange. Find ways to link your position with its performance in those areas.

- **Make yourself indispensable:** Make friends with key players in other departments and volunteer for cross-functional projects. If your job is considered a company expense, look for ways to create profitable activities.

- **Show up:** This isn't the time to shrink into your cube or office. Stop to see people in your group and other departments. Go to all relevant meetings and demonstrate through your words and actions that you are committed to the company's long-term vision.

- **Don't feel guilty:** It's not a crime to survive a round of layoffs, but it's also common to feel survivor's guilt when you come to work and see only darkened cubicles and empty desks. Remember, it's not your fault. Don't let your feelings of responsibility sabotage your effectiveness and career. Use this as an opportunity to expand your skills and value to the company.

- **Stay in touch with those who are laid off:** Don't loose valuable relationships for staffing your Bodacious Career. Those who have been laid off are now out in the big wide world, making new contacts, and sending their careers in new directions. You may have a need for their talent in the future or they may need yours. You never know, they may join a company that provides a business-to-business selling opportunity.

- **Decide whether you want to stay:** After several months or even a year in a post-layoff period, the company environment or mission may be so different that you feel it's no longer a good fit for you. This is the time to remember that in the Now Economy, we're all unrestricted, free agents, giving our valuable talent in exchange for a paycheck and meaningful career. We can choose to stay just as much as the company can choose to ask us to leave. Because it's usually easier to find the next opportunity while you're still working in the current one, try to line up that next job before you hand in your notice. Leave on a positive note.

The Art of Quitting Well

Knowing when and how to leave a company is an art in the Now Economy. With constant change, there's always a cycle of beginning and ending. We love beginnings and the fresh energy that comes with them. We often hate endings and shy away from them, dealing with them only when forced to. Even if you hate your job and can't wait to get away, there's almost always a feeling of loss from the separation. You just want it over with. However, you benefit yourself and others by bringing proper closure to your connection.

Quitting well is an art, not a science. Here are some ideas about how to be a brilliant quit artist:

- **Leave on the best possible terms to help you in the future:** Your involvement with a company is part of your employment history. If you leave on good terms, you increase the chances of getting positive references for future employers or clients. Who knows, your former employer might be a client one day.

- **Don't try to resolve any negative emotions through the quitting process:** You probably won't get any lasting satisfaction from storming into your boss' office and exclaiming, "I'm outta here!" Momentary pleasure, yes, lasting, no.

- **Deal with any ill feelings through out-of-office means:** Talk it out with a friend, take some time away, write a flame letter and then ball it up and throw it across the room. Your best revenge is leaving and being happier elsewhere.

- **Show respect:** Inform your direct manager before anyone else.

- **Plan for individual partings:** Ask those who have been most meaningful to you to meet one-on-one for lunch, dinner, over coffee or otherwise. Just by asking, you've communicated how much you appreciate them, and they'll likely make time for you.

- **Make your last words count:** Emphasize the positive when saying goodbye; focus on something you appreciated, some benefit you gained from your association with that company or person, and something positive about your future. Short and sweet works well and is memorable.

- **Tell people how to get in touch with you:** Give your contact information to those you want to stay in touch with and be the first one to reach out and say hello once you've left.

How to Interview in the Now Economy

What we can often forget when we're not living bodaciously is that when you're looking for a new job, you're interviewing the company as much as they're interviewing you. It's about match and exchange. Do they have what you want? Do you have what they want?

If you feel desperate for a job, you've already put yourself at a disadvantage. Everything about the company, position, and people may look a lot rosier than it probably is. You're much more vulnerable taking whatever's offered rather than assessing the situation for real, personal satisfaction. The same can happen if the company is desperate for you. They may view your abilities to be greater than they are, and you may end up in a spot where it's tough for you to succeed. Or they may spin the company's situation so optimistically, they don't see their own problems, nor do you.

In the Now Economy, you need to get an accurate picture of the company's situation to make your best decision. The bottom line: You have to think like someone investing in or buying the business as well as someone working within it. Before any interview, do your homework. Check stock market performance (if the company is public, of course). How have they done the last few quarters, the last year? What's the stock price trend over the last few years? Do they have a track record of hitting performance targets? Check out the company's Web site for quarterly and annual reports. Even if you can't understand the spreadsheets, read the descriptive overview. What markets are they in? What are their products or services? Who are their competitors? How do competitors rank against them? Do they have a track record of growth and performance? At what evolutionary stage are they, start-up, high-growth, mature or past peak? How is the CEO portrayed? If it's a private company, find articles on the Web from the last twelve months to help you. Also, ask around. Perhaps you'll uncover a reputation or insight you wouldn't know otherwise.

Come to the interview prepared with questions to ask as well as answers to give. Here are some suggestions for new questions to ask in the Now Economy and what to listen for in the responses.

- **What's been the company's growth the last three to five years?** Wall Street measures growth by financial numbers, typically revenues or profits. If they tell you only the customer or production growth, they may be avoiding the fact that profits didn't increase. Do they portray company growth the same as you found in your research? If not, what is this telling you?

- **What improvements or innovations has the company made in the past few years to remain competitive?** Listen for a proactive stance on change and innovation as needed in today's market, both internally and externally. Standing still is not an option for thriving in the Now Economy.

- **Who are your competitors and how do you rank against them?** Listen for solid company knowledge of the competition. Every company has competition, so who are they? Besides, such information may benefit you if you want to check out opportunities at other companies.

- **Where does the company see itself in the next two to three years?** How will it get there? If the company doesn't have a clear sense of direction and strategic plan for the next few years, the ones following will be even more in question. Listen for a clear vision and mission with a specific strategy that spells out where they want to go. Does it make sense to you? Does it seem achievable from what you can tell? Did the company achieve their strategic goals the last two to three years?

- **What three words would you use to describe the company's culture?** Every company has one, and just like a country's culture, it influences everything that happens there. Listen for a quick, positive response that would indicate the culture is strong and perceived positively. A hesitant response may indicate that the person doesn't want to share his or her immediate thoughts. Their culture is the environment you'll live in if you work there. Do you like what you hear? Is it a good match to your personal style?

- **What is the average tenure of your employees?** Tenures of two years or less may indicate an internal problem that isn't clear on the outside. Tenures of 10 years or more may indicate this is a great place to work, but they also may tip you off to internal stagnation or lack of upward mobility.

- **What is the company's employee turnover rate?** How much of this is voluntary? Listen for anything over 15 percent. Twenty percent means one out of every five people is leaving each year. What's wrong with this place? The exception might be a specific industry. For example, front-line customer

service jobs can have a turnover rate of 40 percent or
more; it's the nature of the job and hourly wage wars
that's responsible.

- **What does the company do to retain employees?**
  We're talking more than benefits here. Smart companies
  know they need more than good benefits to keep good
  performers. Listen for common benefits plus elements of
  a company retention strategy, such as additional benefits
  to help juggle other aspects of your life, a results oriented
  culture or employee development programs. Do they offer
  childcare? A fitness center? Onsite banking? Postal service?
  Flex time? Telecommuting? Bonuses? Opinion Surveys?

How to Evaluate Job Offers

Congratulations, you got a job offer, maybe even several! Don't
let flattery overcome your ability to assess and analyze. Enjoy the
attention, let it pump your ego, but don't let it take you on a ride
somewhere don't want to go. Consider what matters most. Here's
one approach; review the factors below and then rank them from
most to least important. If you have trouble deciding which factors
are most important, pay attention to your initial gut reaction to each
topic; you *will* have one, so listen and trust yourself. Don't engage
in mental "shoulds" or outside opinions. There are no right answers,
just best answers for you. You're the one who has to live with the
job, and you won't do well if you're going against yourself.

After you've ranked the factors, compare each job offer against your
list. Which ones match with your top factors? Of those, which ones
best match with the remaining factors? This will help the best
choice become clear. Remember that no company, position or offer
is perfect, so you won't get absolutely everything you want. You may
have to trade some job security for exciting work, for example. The
bodacious way is to be fully aware of your choice and how you
made it.

- **Job security:** That's truly an oxymoron in the Now Economy, but perhaps what you need more than anything is stability from a company. If it looks like this company is likely to be around longer than others and will supply you with needed income, then maybe this is the one to choose. No company is a sure bet, but some don't demand nearly the risk tolerance that others do.

- **Interesting work:** Maybe the only thing that gets your mojo working is variety and new challenges. You want to be continually stimulated and challenged to improve your skills and expand your professional experience. In fact, you need to be passionate about your job.

- **Career Growth:** You want to expand your skills and abilities, and you want a company that that supports your ambition. You want serious opportunity to attend training, conferences, and get on projects that will cause you to stretch. You also want the ability to move up or over to enhance your career.

- **Money:** Whether it's the status, freedom or things you can buy (or bought and have to pay for), money is at the top of your list – THE top. You're willing to go the extra mile for the job if you're well compensated.

- **Rank:** You're aspiring to a certain level in an organization. Above all, title matters, even within a small organization. You want that positional power and are willing to downgrade other factors to get it.

- **Environment:** You've worked in some places where people just didn't treat each other well and the employer set a negative tone. Now it's imperative to have an atmosphere where the employer is positive and people like coming to work.

- **Autonomy:** If you don't have some elbow room in making decisions on the job, you'll go nuts! Not mundane decisions either but real decisions about budgets, projects or working with customers.

- **Personal time:** You are willing to work hard and do your part, but you don't want 70-hour weeks for months or years on end. Your time away from work is particularly important to you, filled with perhaps little league games, recitals, charity work, concerts, cooking, game fishing, sailing, collecting stamps, you name it. The important thing is that there's plenty of time out of the office to call your own.

- **Travel:** Or lack of travel. You want to see the country or the world, and a job is your travel ticket. Or perhaps you've seen enough hotel rooms and want to stay in one same place. Either way, how much the job requires travel is a big deal.

- **Other:** There are many factors to consider. Fill in the blanks as needed. Decide what topic helps you sort out what's most important so you can choose the offer that best suits you.

What Most Employers Don't Want You to Know When They Talk Salary

When it comes to negotiating a salary package, most working women are clueless. The good girl mode kicks in under pressure. We're afraid of looking too aggressive, ungrateful, greedy or full of ourselves. We are just grateful for the offer. It goes against our social training to go after a better compensation and benefits package. In fact, it doesn't even occur to most of us.

When hiring managers describe a salary and benefits package to you, they have one main objective in mind; to get the best possible talent for the least possible expense. They're not going to volunteer the fact that they can go higher in salary or negotiate concessions in your benefits package. Here are some things to keep in mind:

- **Salary:** Well-managed companies conduct regular labor market assessments to determine if their salaries are competitive. They use this information to adjust their established pay ranges for each position. Because payroll is one of the biggest expenses of running a business, they often offer you the lowest salary possible and hope to keep you satisfied.

  What they want you to know: It's their philosophy to pay competitively. They want you to feel that your skills and abilities are valued so you will produce good work.

  What they don't want you to know: How your own salary compares with the established pay range. Don't assume it's within the range. Generally, if your hiring manager thinks you will be satisfied with a salary below the pay range, he or she will extend the initial offer below that spread. Remember, the employer's first offer is the *beginning* of your negotiation discussion, not the end of it. Consult these Web sites for more information on salaries and ranges:

  www.salary.com

  www.salaryexpert.com

  www.ecomponline.com

  Always ask for more than the initial offer, even if it's only $2,000 or $3,000 more. Why? You'll communicate to them that you highly value yourself and the contributions you can offer their company. This will send the company the signal to value you as well.

- **Bonuses, Commissions and Merit Increases:** Find out if the company has a bonus or commission plan. Every company handles these plans differently, if they have a plan at all. Most companies include merit increases as part of their performance review system. Find out what the review process is, how performance is measured and rewarded, and what range of increase you could expect. Can you get reviewed earlier for a mid-year increase if your initial salary isn't as high as you'd like? If there is a high demand for your profession, you should also ask for a signing bonus.

- **Benefits:** Benefits are like money in your pocket. Consider them carefully and in detail as you balance the entire compensation package. You can expect to get as much as another third of the value of your salary provided in benefits. There are the basics, such as health insurance and paid sick and vacation leave. There are often additional perks such as child care and 401K plans with matching contributions. You might be able to negotiate other benefits that aren't named, such as paid tuition, company car or car allowance, health club membership or additional time off.

- **Make the Negotiation Work For You:** Know your worth. Don't be shy. Don't appear desperate. Don't worry about appearing greedy. Focus on your confidence as a performer. Know what you want and get the agreement in writing.

So, You've Got the Job. Now What?

Getting the job you want is the first step to the next evolution of your Bodacious Career. Don't wait for your new boss and colleagues to make you feel comfortable or give direction. That's what often happens and, as a result, we usually feel things are off to a slow start. Instead, reach out to them first. You'll already be on your way to creating the relationships and political support you'll need to succeed at your new company.

THE FIRST DAY

- **Go to the company's orientation meeting:** Listen to how the company portrays itself in written materials as well as the people who present them. What are the underlying cultural messages and values? Are they consistent with what you know of the company so far? What behaviors does the company expect of employees? Does the company have a process for letting employees know what managers expect from them such as a performance management or appraisal system? The sooner you understand what's really valued, the sooner you'll know how things really operate and how you can use this informal system for yourself. By all means, ask as many questions as you need to be clear.

- **Reach out to your new boss:** If he or she has not initiated first contact on your first day, ask for a brief meeting. Your purpose is to confirm that you're glad to be there, to reiterate that you plan to add real value to the team, and to express your desire to be clear on your objectives for the first six months.

- **Introduce yourself to everyone in your department:** Greet everyone, from receptionists to administrative assistants to technicians, managers and senior managers. This is your opportunity to create the best first impression. It's not hard to make the first move. Simply state your name, your role, and that you want to say hello. Then ask about the other person's role. Undoubtedly, you will get a smile in return because you've communicated interest by this simple, friendly gesture. You are building relationships that may be key to your success there.

THE FIRST WEEK

- **Determine with your boss specific goals for the first six months:** You want a clear understanding so there's no confusion about your performance. Ask what the perfect result or outcome looks like. Be clear on any resources or restrictions. Make sure you show progress or results quickly to confirm your abilities and contribution.

- **Have lunch with at least three different people in your group:** The first-day introduction was a good start; now build on it by initiating a more significant interaction. Make it easy for others by asking lots of questions that get them to talk about themselves.

- **Get all your logistics set up:** You need these tools to function, so get started on setting up your phone number, voice mail, computer, network logins, e-mail account, postal mailbox, name badge, parking permit, office supplies, and business cards. Give your phone number and e-mail address to your group and others outside the office.

THE FIRST SIX MONTHS

- **Perform:** Deliver on agreed-upon results. Generate at least one or two innovative ideas tied to significant department goals. Gain as much new business knowledge as you can. Ooze competence.

- **Get feedback from your boss:** How satisfied is he or she with your results? How can you improve? Listen carefully to comments about what you've produced, and be professional and positive in your response.

- **Try to get in front of your boss' boss:** It's much easier to give a fresh impression as the new hire than to be someone unknown who's been around a while. Come up with an idea or information to share tied to an objective this person is trying to achieve, then ask for a chance to discuss it. Don't be shy about showing up your boss; simply make him or her look good in the process.

- **Continue netconnecting:** Expand beyond your department. Reach out to others in meetings or on project teams. Understand who's who and what role they play. Share about yourself.

- **Assess the power structure:** What is political power based upon – knowledge, creativity, position, results, personal presence? Figure out who's got it, how people get it, and how to use it to help you. (More on this in Chapter Five, *Embrace Office Politics.*)

THE FIRST YEAR

- **Continue performing:** In the Now Economy, your ability to consistently produce results will keep you in the driver's seat.

- **Try to be a part of at least one key project that gets you noticed:** Be able to articulate how the project ties to the company's larger objectives or strategy and how your contribution fits. Openly commend others on the project who achieved results alongside you.

- **Propose personal development such as training or attending conferences:** Continuous learning is key in the Now Economy, so upgrade your knowledge and skills where appropriate. Don't let tight budgets get in the way. Get creative! Offer to pay the airfare for an out of town conference that can be combined with a personal vacation. Consider lower cost options such as regional events or online courses.

- **Continue building your external network:** Change is the norm of the Now Economy, so you need to be able to shift as circumstances change. Initiate chats with those outside of your company. You never know who may be your next employer or client. Keep your options open.

Embrace Office Politics

- When you think of office politics, does anything positive come to mind?

- Are you engaged in office politics without realizing it?

- How can you use office politics to help achieve your goals?

- Do you know the power bases in your company?

One Thing I Wish I'd Understood Before I Quit AOL

I try not to dwell on this too much. But had I known this sooner, this little bit of intelligence may have prevented a lot of angst and propelled my career to even higher levels: *Office politics can be a good thing.*

Surprised? So was I. If I had been a little more savvy about how I could make office politics work for me, I might have avoided the glass ceiling and stayed at AOL a little longer. I might have achieved the title of director or even vice president. I would have understood better what my boss meant when he said, "Mary, you're just not strategic enough. He passed me over for a promotion and gave the job I was over-qualified for to an outsider. In fact, he never would have had to say that because I would have scoped out well in advance what behaviors he particularly valued and performed those behaviors to my advantage in addition to my stated job requirements. Now *that* would have been strategic!

But no. For 10 years, I operated as though my job was to get the work done with passion and to be a team player in helping AOL realize its big vision: "To build an interactive medium that improves the lives of people and benefits society as no other medium before it."

That's a pretty tall order, if you ask me. Wasn't it enough that I was helping the company change the world without focusing on distracting, petty little power plays? I mean, really, there are only so many hours in the day! Well, the fact of the matter was, those power plays were happening all around me whether I liked it or not. And by not bodaciously engaging in them, I wasn't able to fully utilize my workplace power.

In my noble naïveté, like a good foot soldier who's not completely concentrating on where she's going, I tripped and fell on my own sword. Was I skewered by someone else's scheming? Was this something to blame someone else for? I don't think so. I was just so focused on the greater mission of the work at hand that I didn't take steps to show my boss that I was also capable of strategizing a plan for the future. I wasn't clued into the fact that this is what it took to impress him. You don't need a nasty conniver to be on the losing side of a political game. Sometimes you just have to be dedicated to your work.

I needed to help my boss regard me in a far more powerful light. That would have required some political strategy, and that's the thing I resisted. Office politics seemed so unworthy, so suspicious, so underhanded. Isn't it enough just to help make AOL the leading

Internet service provider on the planet? Guess not! I also needed to get smart about office politics. And I didn't realize that until it was too late.

Office Politics Aren't Always Pretty, but Snow White and Sleeping Beauty Are

How much would you trust a woman who brags, "I just love office politics!" Not very much, I'd bet. Even I would be very careful about what I said to her. But office politics can be a powerful, positive tool for your Bodacious Career.

Sometimes office politics aren't pretty. It goes against our good girl coding of being kind, accommodating, self-sacrificing, and forthright. The only behavioral sleight of hand our culture allows women is just a touch of romantic trickery. In fact, a woman who is perceived as especially good at office politics is usually vilified. She's categorized as scheming, conniving, untrustworthy, self-centered, opportunistic – all those words that especially go against the good girl grain. For hundreds of years, in fact, to describe a woman as ambitious was not flattering.

How awful it would be for our coworkers to mistrust us and our core motives! Wouldn't it be better for us to be virtuous, simple, trusted, and just plain good at what we do, regardless of the sacrifice of our potential growth? And worse, how awful it would be if we actually tried to pull a fast one and failed! It would be the cosmic comeuppance. We'd have to endure those whispers behind our back: "She got what she deserved." It's so much better to play it safe, play it good, and, as a result, play it with self-imposed limitations.

It's not surprising that most of us don't know how to engage in politics. Think of our earliest models of women, for instance, Sleeping Beauty and Snow White. They were celebrated for their gentle, innocent presence. In fact, at least according to the Disney version, so innocent, so trustworthy, so harmless were they that they moved through life completely oblivious to anything wicked happening around them. Their very goodness and physical beauty was their meal ticket. Each was admired and trusted by the creatures of the forest. Sleeping Beauty and Snow White led such angelic lives in the beginning, but we all know what happened to them; they both got snookered by ambitious wicked witches.

I'd also like to point out here that most of the creatures of the Disney forest were gentle vegetarians: the bunnies, the deer, the squirrels, the birdies, all of whom are at the bottom of the forest's organizational food chain. Now imagine Sleeping Beauty waltzing with a grizzly! How great it would be to command the respect of a creature that could reduce you to a quivering lump with one swipe of a paw. Now that would have been bodacious!

So here they are hanging out with what is basically the Animal Kingdom's support staff and misfits (those seven guys aren't exactly fast-track material), not having their potential tested in any challenging way, and counting on their beauty and youthful innocence to get them what they wanted to lead fulfilling lives. They were definitely not bodacious.

Soon they fall into the evil hands of ambition. Snow White's nemesis is jealous of her beauty and comes up with the apple gambit. Now Snow, in her innocence bites into the apple and is thus iced until Prince Charming happens by with pre-heated lips.

Sleeping Beauty has a slightly more bodacious and political twist. In fact, this might be the young girl's first introduction to a little wink-wink, nod-nod workplace political intrigue. Here we are at the princess's first birthday party, the power reception of the year. Everyone who's anyone is invited, except for one; the wicked witch. Some people are so touchy! Of course, she comes anyway. Eleven fairies step up to the crib and bestow on the baby all the virtues necessary to flesh out any princess' resume; looks, smarts, wit, cash. The youngest fairy, having procrastinated, has nothing to offer (not a good career move). So she lets the wicked witch announce her gift next. Well, the witch totally vents, says something pretty threatening about a prick and a demise and then flounces off in a snit.

Now this is where the youngest fairy gets political. It's actually the best part of the story. She waits until the witch is out of hearing distance and then addresses the assembled party (which, of course, really isn't so much of an assembled party anymore – there's nothing like a curse to ruin everything), saying, "Look, I can't do much about the curse. That's over my head. But I can reduce the fine just a tad. Instead of the princess being dead for, like, ever, let's make it, say, 100 years, okay? And just so you don't miss anything, I'll knock everyone out on their 21st birthday and lock up the place with some briars. After a century has gone by, a prince will come along, break the spell and everyone will rise and shine. The yardman might have some cleaning up to do, but that's about it. In the meantime, keep Her Highness away from sharp things. How's that?"

This is a very bodacious and political fairy. She waits until the coast is clear to make her move. She doesn't pause to ask permission. She leverages her talents to their utmost capacity, she dares to change the course of events launched by someone farther up the organizational chart and she courageously speaks up before the entire community. She puts her little fairy foot down, and says, "No! The future will not go that way, it will go this way!"

Talk about garnering some major points with the king!

The youngest fairy is the best part of the story. But we tend to dismiss her contributions as just a really nice thing she did; one of those nurturing, caretaking services all women are expected to perform. We overlook her while marveling at the wicked witch's evil connivings, the princess' beauty, and the prince's dashing heroics. What this fairy did was political, pure and simple. And she saved the day! But if she came up to you in your cube and confided, "I just love office politics, don't you?" You'd probably make a mental note not to invite her to any of your parties. I know I would. But think what would have happened without her!

Politics is Relationships Plus Power

Office politics is really about relationships plus power. I'm all for good relationships at work, most women are. Staffing my Bodacious Career involves creating deliberate relationships that can help me move forward and minimize the effects negative people can have. Sometimes this is a challenge, but all in all, it doesn't press my good girl buttons. But, power, that's another story! It's evil, right? Well, it can be. It's not as if we don't have enough stories about power being abusive, harmful or strictly self-serving. That's one side of power. But there's another side of power that's positive.

Let's be real: Every workplace is political, and the higher up the organizational chart you go, the more political the workplace gets. That's because there's more at stake. The higher up you go, the more things get accomplished by virtue of relationships and positioning. Think about it. Entry-level, front-line positions, such as customer service reps and junior programmers typically don't get caught up in high-level, complex positioning and angling for power. To them, serving the customer or writing code is job one-and-only. In a very important way, the company vision is never so clear and pure as at that level. It's usually as one rises through the ranks that ego, hidden agenda, and compromise begin to show up. As there's more to gain, there's also more to lose. And everyone is doing what's necessary to make sure they don't lose.

Bodacious Women know this: The higher up you go in an organization, the more office politics you get. They also know that the question isn't whether to play, but how.

Here's some more news: "Office politics" is just another way of spelling "leadership". And that's a good thing! Like leadership, political acumen is the artful technique of making people feel good about themselves while they are helping you. It is a form of plugged-in power that is created when we are trusted and have built a track record that says, "You can count on me." We may use the strategies of office politics to gain a competitive advantage in our own careers, but in most cases, we gain from office politics only if what we do ultimately benefits the company, its employees, and stakeholders.

On a day-to-day basis, office politics can:

- Allow people at all levels of the organization to move up and around, because politics can give individuals the opportunity to get recognized.

- Help managers support their employees through acquiring the resources they need to get the job done and serve as a buffer between the employees and pressures from higher-ups.

- Help the company as a whole succeed as senior level leaders use politics to cultivate support and enthusiasm for company initiatives.

But, like anything misused or used to the extreme, politics have a downside. In an unhealthy political environment that breeds distrust, politics can:

- Focus employees inward to protect their own turf rather than outward on the customer. The customer suffers and the company's overall health is diminished.

- Put too much focus on form and image and take the emphasis away from substance and content. Without substance, investors and employees rapidly lose their faith in the company.

- Deprive just reward to people who are so focused on contributing to an organization's success, that they neglect their personal clout and competitive position inside the company.

That's an easy mistake to make, especially in a company where the mission is so all-absorbing and demanding. And in AOL's early days, I made that mistake. The trouble was that, to some extent, I continued to make it.

Side Bar

Is Someone Playing Power Games With You?

The Bodacious Woman knows the more power she possesses, the more others are going to want that power. Her bodacious friends will ask her for favors and advice, but unbodacious people will try to steal power from her. So the Bodacious Woman needs to be alert to these subtle (or not so subtle) power games:

- Someone initiates a meeting with you but insists that you come to his or her office. If the person is your boss or ranks higher in the organization, this is appropriate. But if the person is your equal or below you, he or she should come to you or you should meet in some neutral territory such as a conference room or cafeteria.

- Someone often keeps you waiting on purpose, but you know it's not just that they're poor at time management.

- Someone repeatedly rejects your ideas and insists on new ones in a rapid-fire, high-pressure atmosphere.

- Someone is always looking down on you. Some people maneuver themselves and their office furniture to make sure they are always at least at eye level or higher than you. They're angling for height advantage because they feel at a disadvantage in other ways.

- Someone touches you too frequently or inappropriately, which sends the message of a one-up-one-down relationship.

- Someone is determined to have a blank expression in response to anything you say. Not showing any expression during a conversation is just plain odd. If you see a poker face on the person you're trying to talk to, you can safely assume he or she wants to keep important thoughts hidden.

How do you respond to these power plays? That's up to your personal style and your relationship with others. It's important that you take a mental step back and notice what's going on and identify strategies to maintain your feelings of confidence and self-worth. (Consider the six characters from Chapter Two that often show up when you take a stand.) This is your bodacious advantage.

(Office) Size Still Matters

From the day I showed up at Quantum in my blue seersucker suit, I leveraged my good girl ethic. Work hard. Be trustworthy. Be fair. Produce. People will notice. And in the early days, they did. That was when the company was simple, at least at the level I was working in. There were so few of us, so the ones who produced got noticed and rewarded. Do an outstanding job and you had your ticket to advancement. Being a good girl worked for me.

It stopped working around 1997, but I was too good a girl to notice. When I finally did, it was too late. One of the biggest and hardest lessons for me was realizing that although those below me in the organization still supported the "perform well and you'll get promoted" rule of behavior, the ones immediately above me were operating according to a different set of rules: "I assume you're going to perform well unless you prove otherwise. What I want to know now is what else can you offer?" My big mistake was that I didn't put the time, energy, and creativity into answering that "what else" question and then promoting myself for all I was worth.

The change in political environment wasn't just about my own upward trek through the power layers. There was an important shift within AOL as well, a shift that affects every start-up as it matures, grows, and finally begins to act like an established company. It was growing up just like I was. I was practically homegrown from within AOL's incubator. After my seven years in this AOL green house, the company was hiring thousands and thousands of new employees who were both professionally competent and politically savvy. I may have had years of organizational knowledge, but I knew little about the buy-and-sell world of power brokering. Compared with the outside experiences these new employees brought to AOL, I had no real sense of the subtext of intrigue and positioning.

For most of those years, that was just fine. My value to the company was in the relationship organizational knowledge, and personal skills I brought to the workplace. I was too busy to realize that I needed to convert these assets into political know-how.

Just how far I was out of touch showed up in 1997 when the AOL campus near the Dulles International Airport was being developed.

Offices and cubicles were assigned, not by efficiency or the amount of space each employee would need, but by title. How ridiculous, I thought!

What a contrast to a few years earlier when my manager, the call center director, preferred to have his workspace in the middle of the floor so he was in the flow of activity and modeling the "we're all in this together" attitude that he wanted from his employees. I knew when his boss finally insisted that he have the largest corner office with windows that we were entering a new phase with a different kind of symbolism. As humans, we tend to want a leader to look up to (and criticize when things don't go well). Prime physical space represented importance. Still, a part of me was saddened by the loss of leadership purity that this new value represented.

Of course, I had my own saga with my office spaces and how they represented my rise and slip within AOL. During my time at AOL, I had over ten workspaces, ranging from open cubicles I shared with others to semi-private cubes and several small and large offices. As I transitioned through them all, I saw the advantage of each situation, but I never allowed myself to connect the space with stature – just the workload and the environment I needed to get it done. I appreciated the privacy of offices when I was creating and writing training materials. I enjoyed the openness and sociability of the cubes when I managed the call center. And by the time I landed an office with a pond view, I began to appreciate what it meant to have such a space. But you know what they say, you don't know what you've got till it's gone.

In losing my bid for the promotion to director, I also lost the wonderful office. The outsider took it over. I realized that once I lost that office and was relegated to the cube outside of it, I would lose some political status.

But losing the office symbolized an even greater loss; I lost the battle to realize my dreams to continue rising through the ranks of a company I cared deeply about. But in a larger sense, I'd won something more valuable: I won the chance to explore a new chapter in my Bodacious Career.

Strategies from the Political Masters

Few like to admit they enjoy office politics, but there is one group of experts who don't mind political intrigue at all and don't mind you knowing it, either; professional politicians. Presidents, Congressional Representatives, Senators, and their various aides and other professionals who play this particular game make no bones about what they do. In fact, they're *expected* to engage in the finer techniques of getting things accomplished through relationships. And their examples are out there for all of us to learn from.

STRATEGY 1: KNOW WHAT WINNING MEANS TO YOU

Bodacious Women ask, "What do you win?" Do you know why you're competing in the first place? What does winning look like to you? Is this particular game worth your time and attention or is there a different game going on somewhere else with better prizes?

Remember the first time you sat down to a board game with your family and you first started hearing talk about winning? "What do I get if I win?" you might have asked. "Nothing," your family probably said. "Just the satisfaction of knowing you're the best player this time." That might have been enough over a friendly game of Candyland. But in the grown-up world, although doing your best certainly still holds personal satisfaction, your concept of winning must be far more compelling and unambiguous. Unless you know what you're playing for and what winning looks like, you may not realize when you're winning.

Depending on the political challenge, you have the opportunity for both micro- and macro-wins. The micro-wins are the short-term prizes that you can see every day or that you can project out a few months into the future. Micro-wins include things like a position for a plum project; a new relationship that opens powerful doors; the opportunity to present to a group of high-level executives; a new, larger, upscale office; an invitation to an important reception with important players or getting your tuition fully reimbursed.

Micro-wins can accumulate to help achieve macro-wins. Macro-wins may include your long-term goals to climb through the ranks and achieve a senior executive position or gain more and more influence in a personally meaningful cause so that you become its prominent spokesperson or become a widely recognized industry expert, giving you a broader field of opportunities.

Investing some regular focus on macro-wins is an important part of your political strategy. This will help you make key decisions as to whether one particularly tempting short-term gain is worth the possible damage to long-term goals. A wrong decision can cause many women to be labeled selfish "bitches" and men to be called wimpy "yes men". Immediate gratification can cost big in terms of long-term benefits. On the other hand, there may be some macro-wins that really could be put off in favor of a booster shot of micro-win benefits.

STRATEGY 2: UNDERSTAND YOUR POWER BASE

The core of office politics is power and how you use it to get things done. How effective you are in office politics is really a reflection of how you leverage the various points of power that are deemed most important by the organization.

Knowledge Power: What You Know

In the Now Economy, knowledge power can bring you the big bucks early in your career, especially in high-tech. AOL and other Internet and high-tech companies pay a premium for qualified technical employees and then treat them like demi-gods. If you're largely motivated by money and have an aptitude for technology, knowledge power is excellent political capital for you to use to invest in your future.

However, you don't have to be a techie to capitalize on your own knowledge power. Here are other kinds of knowledge power that will give you political leverage on the job:

- **Organizational knowledge:** This is power I could have leveraged more. After 10 years at AOL, I was like Radar O'Reilly on M*A*S*H. I knew how to get just about anything anyone needed. I knew tons of people and I knew both the written and unwritten rules about how things were done. It's because of my organizational knowledge that I was asked to find a way to get a high response rate to the company's first employee opinion survey. I remember my boss saying, "Mary, you know how this place works better than anyone else. Make it happen." And I did.

- **Content Knowledge:** If you are able to find a passion early and steep yourself in it as a child, by the time you're ready to market that passion commercially, you've outpaced your competition before you even start. Think about filmmakers like Steven Spielberg and Ron Howard. By the time they were young men, they were ready to hit the ground running. But if you're like most people, it's taken time and some meandering down different paths to find your passion. Once you find it, you can't help wanting to learn everything you can. You don't have to throw out what you've learned to date, you can often apply previous knowledge to the expertise you're gaining.

• **Industry Knowledge:** Maybe you're not intrigued by a certain subject matter, but you fully understand how a particular industry works. You know the ropes, how business is transacted, who the key players are, how to favorably position a company or product or service, what the industry trends are, and how to close deals. You love the process of bringing all the elements together to make things happen. That's powerful! Your knowledge is golden because it's the way business often gets done.

• **Behavioral Knowledge:** There's power in knowing how people prefer to be treated. If your former boss liked to have weekly progress reports but your current boss despises them, how happy do you think he'd be if you continued behaving in the old way? Or maybe you know when making presentations to a certain executive that she likes to see headlines first followed by the details. Gaining behavioral knowledge requires paying close attention to others and not letting your preferences get in the way. When you apply these behavioral insights, they can become a powerful asset.

Creative Power: How You Apply What You Know

Knowledge is like a great computer or kitchen appliance. It may look pretty and impressive, but it won't do a darn bit of good until you plug it in. The ways you apply what you know from what company you choose to work for to how you help launch a new product to how you solve a customer's problem, makes the difference between being known for getting results and being a box on an organizational chart. How we move forward depends on how creatively we reassemble bits and pieces of ideas and facts we hear every day and apply our knowledge to come up with effective ideas.

Roomfuls of data are completely meaningless if you don't have fresh, valuable ways to apply that data and bring it to market. Cultivate a reputation as a smart, creative person, and you will garner political power. People will always want to know what's on your mind.

Positional Power: What Your Rank Is

Your job title can open doors. The company you work for may also be a name that opens doors. But you have to be willing to use that position as leverage to make things happen for you. It doesn't matter where you're positioned in your company, there will be people who look to you precisely for the role you play, your access to
certain people, and your unique ability to make things happen in your particular corner. Remember, if your position isn't vital to the business, it wouldn't have been created. If you hadn't been the best candidate for that position, you wouldn't have been hired for it. If you have risen through the ranks, you have more than earned your position. It belongs to you. You've proven yourself again and again. So claim the political power that comes with it – and use it!

Side Bar
Power Moves: Behaviors That Communicate Strength

I'm convinced there are mannerisms and behaviors women use that lessen power rather than increase it. Trouble is, most women aren't paying attention to the difference. As a result, they are much less empowered than they need to be. Here are some basic power moves that communicate strength:

- **Bodacious Women don't end every sentence with a question mark?** Have you noticed that many women make a sentence into a question as if they want you to agree because they're uncertain of their facts and opinions? I wouldn't feel comfortable putting them in charge of a strategically important project? I probably wouldn't even trust them to competently answer the most basic questions about the business? Would you?

- **Bodacious Women keep their hands out of their hair.** And away from their face. And they don't fidget with their pens while talking. Nervous gestures send the signal that you're not certain of your own opinions or are feeling intimidated or nervous.

- **Bodacious Women don't over-complain or over-explain.** Katharine Hepburn once said, "Never complain, never explain." Katharine Hepburn is a prime example of bodaciousness, someone we can all aspire to be. I don't know anyone who can get through life without complaining just a little bit now and then or without having to explain something every once in a while. But generally, women tend to over-complain and over-explain. We put ourselves on the defensive by constantly feeling as though we must be accountable about where we are, why we're there, what we're thinking, and how we arrived to that conclusion. You owe the world results, not an explanation.

- **Bodacious Women choose their vocabulary.** Some words are more powerful than others. Trendy expressions, such as, "I was like..." or "Hello???" or "Whatever," aren't very powerful so the best thing is to use them sparingly for effect. Swearing may get attention but is generally considered unprofessional no matter the person's rank or gender. Although, what the hell, it can be effective now and then! If you laughed just now and got the point, it's because humor is a very powerful communication technique, too. But, watch out! Humor can work against you when used to put down others. Lastly, it always works to your advantage to use terms common to the audience or group. If you know some people aren't familiar with a term or concept, then mixing in laymen language is very effective.

- **Bodacious Women dress and act as though they already have the power of the next step up.** In my first position at AOL as a call center rep, I often dressed more professionally than my colleagues. People in other departments thought I was a supervisor or manager because of it. It was a huge lesson in how dress affects how you're perceived. Fashion experts advise you to dress for the job you want to have. Given the more casual workplace environment of the Now Economy, that's not always so easy to do. But you can act with the confidence positional power brings. Work with as much confidence and autonomy as you can. Consider those higher up the organizational chart as equals and relate to them accordingly. This is the power of positioning.

- **Bodacious Women notice achievements and give positive feedback**. The old management model said, "If you don't hear from me you'll know I'm satisfied." But in the highly creative, high-stakes atmosphere of Now Economy business, your co-workers – even those above you in the hierarchy – want to know you recognize and appreciate their efforts. People who do this easily are emotionally attractive. Gaining good favor is powerful.

Relationship Power: Who You Know

"It isn't what you know it's who you know" is a common saying, sometimes delivered with irony, resentment, sarcasm and cynicism. What is so wrong with leveraging your contacts and the power that comes with them? That's what staffing your Bodacious Career is all about (Want a review? Check out Chapter Two again.) Additionally, it's great to be part of a workplace community that recognizes individual contributions. More than ever before, we can bring our true selves to the workplace and impact our associates' hearts with our authenticity and effectiveness. One of the best aspects of relationship power is that it goes both ways, power is shared, and both parties benefit.

Personal Power: Your Relationship With Yourself

It's not the successful presentation before the executive team that makes or breaks dreams, nor is it the meant-to-be job interview. The first hurdle for success happens between your ears. Does your self-talk routinely dismantle every good idea you have and discourage you from making it known? If it does, you can take comfort in knowing that you're not alone. But remember, there's no future in self-sabotage.

Our self-esteem can be one of the biggest barriers to achieving careers that capitalize on our entire potential, pay us what we're worth, and broaden our horizons. Do any of the following ring a familiar mental bell?

"I don't feel right pointing out my accomplishments. That sounds like bragging to me."

"Maybe I'd get more respect if I looked better."

"What did I say that would cause him to turn on me like that?"

"In some ways, it would have been better if I had lost the job instead of my friend. She needs the work more than I do."

"I get embarrassed too easily for myself and others."

"I shouldn't have applied for that new position.
I haven't worked hard enough."

Alan Weiss, author of *Million Dollar Consulting*, says this: "Your first sale must be to yourself." If you're not a happy customer, perhaps you've allowed yourself to be negative for too long. It's up to you to replace your self-defeating thoughts and beliefs with new, positive messages. Going to counseling, talking with a trusted friend, and journaling are just a few ways you can start the process. A positive relationship with yourself is fundamental to stepping onto the bodacious world stage. Looking for help isn't a sign of weakness, you're just taking another step toward the authentic self you deserve and need to be.

STRATEGY 3: KNOW YOUR PLATFORM

Politicians know what they stand for – at least what they stand for now. You can always change when it's strategically wise to do so, as long it's an authentic change. Famous politicians have been known to change parties; Ronald Reagan was once a Democrat and Hillary Rodham Clinton started out as a Republican.

The old expression goes like this: "Know what you stand for or you'll fall for anything." Knowing what you stand for, and then letting others know it too, is an important aspect of personal branding. What do you stand for in your career, no non-sense strategies that make a difference to the bottom line, identifying new products or services by analyzing trends, helping your company develop family-friendly human resource policies or working for a company that is environmentally friendly?

What is your "domestic" policy? What do you stand for within the workplace? Can people count on you to keep a secret, to respect deadlines and go to bat for them when their own issues are at stake? Are you known for being fair and open? What's your reputation with others and is this in line with your personal brand? (Check out the side bar *10 Things You Want Your Reputation to Say About You* in Chapter Two.)

When you know what your platform is, market it! Obviously you can't stand at the back end of a train car speaking into a microphone before a cheering crowd. But there are excellent and effective ways to push your message forward and position yourself in just the right spotlight:

- When distributing progress reports, tie your accomplishments to your platform whenever possible.

- Use your e-mail signature line to publish a favorite quote that summarizes your perspective or brand.

- Lend meaningful books to friends on subjects important to you. For instance, I would never have latched on to the concept of being bodacious, if it wasn't for Tiane Mitchell-Gordon at AOL who shared with me two of her favorite books by SARK, who celebrates the bodacious life.

- Be willing to give presentations on topics that are of interest to others and for which you want to be known.

STRATEGY 4: LEARN THE ART OF LOBBYING

How do you suppose all those elected officials come to understand the intricate details of controversies, issues, and national policies? Hired experts prowl the halls of the legislative offices throughout the country (not just Washington, DC) and grab these policy makers every chance they get to learn about another insight or message. This is why they're called lobbyists; they used to hang out in the lobbies of congressional office buildings and wait to get legislators' attention.

Today lobbying is done much the same way, although in a much more sophisticated manner by holding receptions, initiating letter-writing and e-mail campaigns, and drawing on the currency of long-standing friendships.

The famous "elevator speech" is an example of lobbying for your Bodacious Career. You can grab the attention of key movers and shakers by having a really good sixty-second explanation of who you are and what you do. Be ready to take advantage of the happenstance meeting in the ladies' room, fitness center or cafeteria. You can also make sure you show up to an event or meeting where you may be able to create the opportunity to speak with someone you'd like to influence. This may sound unseemly and scheming, but it's not if it's something important to you. Just be sure you can sleep at night and face yourself in the mirror the next day.

STRATEGY 5: LEARN THE ART OF COMPROMISE

You may not be able to get all that you want so know what you're willing to settle for. Know the difference between your non-negotiables and negotiables. Would you be willing to forego the well-earned bonus this time if you knew you'd get a bigger bonus once the new contract comes through? Do you have the nerve to ask for that deal in writing?

You may not get everything you want in a certain arrangement, but you will get some of what you want if you learn to compromise. Learn to compromise well, and the part that you do get will be what you wanted most.

STRATEGY 6: LEARN GRACEFUL DEFEAT

Sometimes, you won't even get part of what you want. It may feel humiliating or devastating. You might even feel betrayed by your boss who said he'd support you and then didn't. You'll feel as though you don't belong in the company anymore. Maybe you'll even start considering grad school!

No defeat is truly an utter, complete defeat. How you carry yourself through the agonizing time of "chin up" could speak volumes about you to powerful people who are watching. The opportunities that might result from a new level of respect and admiration could be better than anything you imagined.

Graceful defeat is helping the person who got the job instead of you become successful. Graceful defeat is pleasantly surprising your boss who is expecting you to be in a huge snit over the disappointment. Graceful defeat is saying through your actions, "I can't do much about the curse, but I can reduce the fine just a tad."

Voodoo Politics

No chapter on office politics would be complete without a little discussion about the bad stuff, the elusive feeling that you're shadow boxing with the devil and that no matter how hard you swing, you end up hurting yourself.

Let's face it, in the world of this kind of bad mojo, you're an amateur. As naïve as this may sound, it's much better for you to focus on what you do best (providing real value to the company or the project) and let the chips fall where they may for the rest. Those who appreciate your work are really the people to count on in your Bodacious Career. Worst case scenario: The evil one manages to scheme and scam all the way to the top of the organization, leaving you and your career in the dust. You know what? If scheming and scamming nets that kind of easy access to the power center, you're better off taking your talents elsewhere anyway. Just be sure to keep your good relationships there intact in case there is a time you ever return as a customer, client or contractor, which is what I would one day do.

To Build Your Bodacious Career...

• Accept office politics as a fact within any organization; embrace its positive potential.

• Do some honest reflection to assess if you've already engaged in office politics without realizing it. For example, are you using your rank to secure resources for your employees?

• Identify the power base(s) within your company or organization. Determine if these power base(s) match well with your talents and values.

• Identify at least one way you could use office politics for the good of the company and your Bodacious Career.

Think Strategically, Act Bodaciously

In Building Your Bodacious Career...

- Do you strategize first and then act later?
- Have you imagined what your future career looks and feels like?
- Have you created a plan to make that future happen?

Bring It On!

If you've been learning and using the skills, techniques, and attitudes I've described to build a Bodacious Career, it's likely you've already had some micro-wins and successes. I call these bodacious moments, otherwise known as BoMos. Good for you! I bet others are noticing these BoMos and at least one person is just dying to ask, "What has gotten *into* you?" It's my wish that you have begun to develop a more calm, confident, and proactive approach to your career, even the areas that have long been especially troublesome or emotionally charged I hope are becoming easier to manage. You know the ones I'm talking about, those situations that keep coming up again and again like a promotion opportunity that keeps passing you over, a political battle you lose out on that you didn't even know you were fighting, the same point in every confrontational situation where you always back down when you wish you had more staying power.

Time to move along. Time to bring it on! Time to use the Bodacious Way to strategically create a future that's satisfying, creative, rewarding, and responsive to the changing Now Economy. By using the techniques I'll describe in this chapter, you'll benefit from a common business process that all companies use to map out their path; the business plan. But this version will be your personal step-by-step strategic action plan that will take you from dreams to reality.

For companies, the business plan is what defines their vision and mission in real and measurable objectives. It identifies steps needed to meet objectives and scopes out financial consequences. Business planning starts with determining objectives. For example, here are some Bodacious Career building objectives that might be in your personal business plan:

- An assignment working and living abroad, say China, England or Australia.

- A more promising career track with an income that matches the value of your contributions.

- A graduate degree.

- A leadership role in your professional association.

- A seat at your company's most senior executive table.

A step-by-step bodacious action plan is required. Your bodacious business plan will give you the foundation needed to navigate the choppy surface of your moods, fluctuating self-esteem or feelings of anxiety. It can give you a stable, steady compass to follow in a calm and thoughtful time so you know will be able to ride rough waters when they appear, never losing sight of the bigger picture.

Your Big, Bodacious Personal Business Plan

Creating a personal business plan may sound odd and over-the-top, but it's useful, and practical, and it gives you a strategic platform on which to build your dream. As with business, the main purpose here is to take steps to make you more effective and efficient with your time and resources. By laying out all the details, you reduce the risk of failure and increase your chances for success. You will be ready for any potential difficulties. Think of the confidence that alone will inspire!

There are three main parts to your personal business plan:

STEP 1: Capture the current state of your situation

STEP 2: Identify what you want your desired future to look like

STEP 3: Determine what you have to do to get there

Let's look at what's involved in each step for creating the Bodacious Career you want.

STEP 1: YOU ARE HERE

Like the maps throughout your favorite mall indicating "You Are Here," Step 1 helps you understand your current situation as thoroughly as possible. It guides you through the process of discovering what you like as much as it helps you identify the circumstances that you want to change. Have you noticed that when you want make a change, you're so focused on the source of your unhappiness that you overlook the areas that give you true satisfaction? You can learn as much from uncovering what brings you satisfaction – perhaps even more, since satisfaction is your goal – than you can by focusing only on what brings you pain. Which would you rather be an expert in?

The essential parts of Step 1 involve taking a hard, honest look at your job, company, and the marketplace where you currently play.

Job Overview

Take stock in your overall position. What is your current job's purpose? Are you satisfied with your effectiveness? What are you doing now that you weren't doing one or two years ago? What new skills have you learned? Does the job still hold meaning for you? Does it support your values? Is the reason why you once said "yes" to the job offer still compelling enough to keep you going to work?

Break your position down into parts. What parts of your job do you enjoy and would want to take with you as your career progresses? What other aspects of your work leave you fatigued or feeling burned out? What tasks make time fly? What tasks cause the day to creep by?

Separate your role from your company or industry. Do you enjoy your profession but wish you could apply it in a different company or industry? Or do you like the company and industry you're in but are ready to expand your role in it? Or would you like to just chuck it all and start all over again?

Review your finances. Is your income satisfactory? Are you paid the salary you know you're worth or is it at least commensurate with similar positions in your market? Is your salary enough to live a comfortable life to do the things you want while being able to plan for the future (your children's education and your own retirement, for instance)?

Make a list of both positive and negative emotions you associate with your current career such as creative satisfaction, fulfillment, frustration, guilt, gratitude, anger, exuberance, or exhaustion. Don't get mired down in those feelings. Take an objective look at them and use them as diagnostic tools. Notice how you feel and objectively consider *why* you're feeling that way. Then ask *why* again and again until you've got your true answer. What do the *whys* tell you about what elements you should carry with you into your future and which ones you can leave behind?

Company Overview

Be clear what your company is about. What is the company's mission and values? Can you support them? Does the company make a product or a service that you are proud of? Does it have a culture that invigorates you or do you dread walking through the front doors every day? Does the company support your development (not just talk but actual support you in the form of training, cool projects, conferences or promotions)? Does it support corporate citizenship values that are meaningful to you, such as flexibility for family demands, community outreach, environmental awareness or diversity considerations?

Consider the competition. Who are your employer's competitors? How does your company stack up against them? Are worthy competitors possible employers to consider as an alternative to your own company or does your company still offer the best career advantages and prestige? An excellent source for identifying your company's closest competitors (especially if you work for a large national corporation) is www.hoovers.com. This site not only lists the main competitors for any publicly traded company, it also provides descriptions of their competitive positioning, names of key officers and executives, and hyperlinks to their Web sites.

Market Overview

Take a look at your company's customers, the people key to the company's existence. Who are your customers? How satisfied are they? Is the number of customers increasing or decreasing, and why? How could this trend affect your role? Can you see the writing on the wall that tells you within a few years your skills or contributions may no longer be in demand? What are the external market conditions that affect the overall vitality of your industry? Is your company about to experience a huge public relations hailstorm, and will the pummeling show up in a decreased stock price or market share?

STEP 2: YOU WILL BE HERE

Now it's time to put reality aside and dream of the future. All the components of Step 2 help you paint the overall picture that answers the question, "Who do I want to become?"

Here is how some of the components of your personal business plan will help you arrive at your answer:

Describe your future state

How will your future career look and feel to you? What will be your role? What will it be like going to work every morning? Will it provide more creative independence? Will the environment be supportive and respectful? Will you have the flexibility you want for caring for your children? Will you be in Paris or Mozambique? Do you prefer the fun and risk of working for a start-up for less money but more stock options – with the idea that you might eventually be positioned to cash in "big time?"

This is the point where it's valuable to invest the time and concentration to examine exactly what's inside your soul bursting to assert itself. Key points are to be honest with yourself, and to look within. We have so many of the answers inside us if we we're willing to ask ourselves the questions and listen to our hearts. This particular stage is too big to try to incorporate into a single chapter. But there are plenty of excellent books to guide you. Among my favorites are *I Could Do Anything If I Only Knew What It Was* and *Live the Life You Love*, both by Barbara Sher, and *The Path* by Laurie Beth Jones.

Identify the critical success factors

What needs to be in place for your success to happen, a supervisor who supports your growth, a company with upward mobility for women, a corporate policy that's family friendly, fellow employees who share the company's vision and are willing to make necessary sacrifices to make things happen, an industry or company that's growing or a larger city where your ideal company is located? Do you need to acquire more skills? Do you need to meet influential people and cultivate their political support? If you're the sole financial support for your home, how dependable must your income be so you can pursue your dreams? Can you retain external help to free up more time? Author Barbara Sher, for instance, urges women to hire housekeeping help as soon as they can afford it, even if that help is once a month. This is a necessity, not an indulgence, says Sher, herself once a struggling single mother living hand-to- mouth. Not only does it free you up from chores that offer no long-term return on your investment, but it also provides badly needed income for other women who are struggling to make ends meet.

STEP 3: GETTING FROM HERE TO THERE

Now that you have been able to paint a picture of your ideal future, it's time to plot a plan for getting there. Step 3 is the difference between getting stuck in emotionalizing your dreams, feeling frustrated that they haven't already happened, and thinking negatively versus staying calm, confident, focused, and productive. Step 3 is what helps you build a plan consistent with your vision while being flexible and resilient in the face of ever-changing times and shifting circumstances.

There are no templates for creating your implementation plan because each person's objectives and circumstances are unique. However, there are some strategies to keep in mind as you put your plan together.

Strategy 1: Reach Out to Those Who've Been There, Done That

You might be saying, "If I knew what steps to take I wouldn't be buying all these expensive how-to books!" Fair enough. So here's the first step: Get advice from people who have already achieved your mission. Any information or piece of advice that you want concerning the path to making your vision a reality already exists! Someone knows the answer! So identify a few people and then call them up or send them an e-mail, requesting an appointment, either on the phone or in person. The worst thing they can do is say no. But, unless we're talking movie stars or anyone else you might read about in *People* magazine, just about anyone will give you 10 minutes. If in those 10 minutes they see your sincerity and enthusiasm, those 10 minutes can easily turn into a half hour, a few more names to contact, and maybe even a job lead. Nothing opens doors faster than a good dose of sincere, smart and thoughtful humanity. You'll find most people quite willing to lend a hand.

So maybe you don't know who these people are and how to get through to them, that's not as difficult as it may seem. Just remember your job is to start looking. Here are a few suggestions for your search:

- Leverage the network you've been building using your bodacious relationship skills. Consider people both inside and outside your current company. Even if they aren't doing what you're aiming for, it's very possible they can refer you to someone they know who's a great match.

- Attend local meetings of your professional association and do some netconnecting. If you don't know what the association is, and if asking around your company doesn't help, research the Web site for the American Society for Association Executives (www.asaenet.org).

- Try connecting with fellow alumni from undergraduate or gradate school. Many colleges and universities have Web sites where you can search for alumni according to geographic area or degree. Also consider any clubs or groups you were involved in that may have directories such as sororities or academic groups.

Strategy 2: Create Dates For Yourself
(Without the Help of a Dating Service!)

Bodacious companies and Bodacious Women work towards achieving goals by a certain date. This is beneficial in a number of ways:

- A timeline gives you deadlines to shoot for.

- A timeline also helps you break down the goal into doable, less intimidating tasks. You can go to bed at night satisfied, fulfilled, and happy that you completed the day's activities that are bringing you closer to your big goal.

- The process of designing the timeline helps you think through all the external factors that affect your deadlines. Just as you might coordinate your summer vacation with the dates when school is out, you can also determine where you're going to attend the next networking business meeting or course.

- The timeline helps you make sure you have plenty of time to reach the goal. Remember that moment when I discovered I only had a few weeks to prepare for my GREs? Timelines can help you avoid those unexpected events.

- Timelines will also give you milestones to celebrate. Don't skip this important step, even if it's just a family spaghetti dinner to celebrate a long day taking the GREs. Celebrations aren't self-indulgent and they don't have to be extravagant. They are important because they remind you you're making progress on your goal and encourage you to keep going.

Strategy 3: Figure Out How To Get Funding

Almost any bodacious ambition will involve money. Obviously companies must consider their budgets when constructing their business plans. You're no different. Budgets help you just the same as timelines do. They're not there to remind you over and over again how much you lack, they're there to guide you in determining how much you have to work with.

There's always a way to get funding for your dream if you're creative and willing to make adjustments. Perhaps you have a mate who is willing to be the primary breadwinner while you scale back to focus on your goal. Or maybe you decide to reduce or rearrange your monthly expenses to free up some cash. Or it could be that your company's human resource department has tuition reimbursement or daycare subsidy programs. Or perhaps you can apply for a grant from a company who sees the public relations value in supporting your endeavor. Design a realistic budget that works for you, and you will have all the money you need to see you through to realizing your vision.

Strategy 4: Ask For The Support You Need

Companies need employees to achieve their business goals. Although you may not have employees to help support you personal business plan, you're likely surrounded by people who will help you reach your goals, many of whom would enjoy pitching in to see you soar. Married or single, children or childless, list those who may be willing to help in some small, meaningful way to lighten your load. Often all it takes it asking! Just ask your:

- husband or significant other to agree to cook the meals (or otherwise figure out dinner. Do I hear take-out?!).

- friend or family member to pick up your younger kids from daycare so you can attend an evening meeting.

- older kids to wash the dishes while you hole up in your room studying for your new class.

- colleagues and associates to act in an advisory capacity, as a board of directors might.

- a weekly housekeeper to keep your environment pleasant and uncluttered so you can concentrate and have time to dedicate to your mission.

There are also those who can help in a big, meaningful way to keep you on track. They're called personal coaches and they're everywhere now! Hiring a personal coach is like having a teammate, someone fully committed to coming alongside to help you stick to achieving your dreams. They're there to spur you on when all is going well and also there to help you keep moving when you're experiencing a speed bump. To find a good coach, ask for referrals from those you respect or you can search for a certified coach through the International Coach Federation (www.coachfederation.org).

Strategy 5: Preach it Sister!

Your vision may be lofty. It may be inspiring. It may save the world. But it won't fly unless you're able to tell the story of your vision to those who can help you achieve it. Companies market themselves in a variety of ways from producing commercials to supporting the arts or education in their communities to cultivating relationships with journalists covering their industry or sponsoring charity events. How you spread the message of your vision is limited only by your imagination and enthusiasm. This is where staffing your Bodacious Career really makes a difference...again.

For example, if your dream is to get promoted to the next level in your company, how do you promote the value of your work to your boss? I wrote weekly reports to my AOL boss that marketed my achievements and value to the department. I also photocopied thank-you letters for a job well done and forwarded similar e-mails to my boss. Notice what areas your boss is over-committed (perhaps a too-full speaking schedule?) and volunteer to take some of that load off his or her shoulders. Don't worry that you might get "scut" work. That may happen at first, still, you're demonstrating that you're willing to do what it takes. Communicate the value of those assignments and ask for better ones.

Consider if evangelizing yourself to other departments helps your goal. If so, introduce yourself to the heads of other departments in a low-key, no-pressure way. Say "hi" to their administrative assistants. Introduce yourself to those you don't know at interdepartmental meetings. Forward articles of interest to others with a note explaining why the article made you think of them and why you think they'd be interested. In all these situations, be prepared to have one or two sentences that market you and listen for how you can tie in with other people's' interests.

Perhaps your goal requires external marketing. In that case, consider joining the key association for your field and your marketplace and regularly attend their meetings. As time allows, be active in their special interest groups (SIGs). You might find a women's leadership SIG, a technical SIG or a marketing SIG. Or check out other business groups that match your external marketing needs.

Strategy 6: Remember to Take Care of YOU!

Companies know how important it is to staff morale and productivity to have a workplace that is safe, attractive, comfortable, and in good working order. Your body is your primary work environment. What kind of condition is it in? It's a question to ask yourself as you're creating your personal business plan, and one to keep asking after you get started. Bodacious dreams take stamina on all levels; physically, mentally, emotionally, and spiritually. It's important to schedule activities to keep yourself healthy and sane; making appointments with the treadmill, going to aerobic or yoga classes, doing meditation or prayer, taking walks, journaling, listening to inspirational tapes, and more. You decide! By taking care of yourself, you are preparing one of the most important tools you need to realize your plan. Ambition takes gumption, fortitude, and stamina. Good health gives you staying power.

Love Every Minute of It!

As companies progress according to their business plans, they pause now and then to reconsider how their needs have changed. You will need to do that as well with your personal business plan. In the Now Economy where you need to thrive on shift and change, you also need to frequently review your plan and make adjustments that take new developments into account. And you need to keep at it. Dreams don't come true overnight and they usually don't manifest without some bumps and twists and turns. Such events will challenge your resolve to make sure you really want to achieve your goal. That's why you need to decide up front that you're going to love every minute of it! You're a woman of courage! You're no longer stuck, you're alive, you're kicking, you're engaged in life!

You're BODACIOUS!

To Build Your Bodacious Career...

Create a personal business plan for your Bodacious Career by doing the following:

• Take a hard, honest look at your currently job, company, and the marketplace. Capture what you like and dislike.

• Determine where you really want to take your career. Dream, brain storm, do some soul searching. Then decide on your next step or goal.

• Build a real, workable plan to make your dream a reality.

Frequently review your plan to make adjustments. Celebrate achievements along the way. Remember to love every minute of it!

Epilogue

The journey to bodaciousness takes courage. It's a process that has many rewarding – as well as retrenching – experiences like the ones I've shared. It involves staring your fears about yourself, about others, about life, in the face. You may wonder sometimes if you can keep on this road. You will also feel more alive than ever before and know you can't turn back. As you press on one foot in front of the other you will mysteriously receive strength to become the bodacious woman you want to be! Don't give up. Life's too short, learn as fast as you can.

When I started with AOL I wasn't bodacious, but when we got done with each other this was what we created. I continue to be grateful for the experiences I had there and that I had the privilege to be an even small part of creating one of the most influential mediums of our time. Since leaving AOL I've applied my bodaciousness to venture into new territory, including completing my master's degree in organization development, becoming an angel investor in the human resources technology and consulting company HumanR, and setting out to write this book. Sometimes I wonder who is this adventurous person living inside my body? Then I realize I'm just getting more used to my new skin.

The Now Economy isn't a fad, it's here to stay. And with all its topsy turvy changes and curves that seem to affect every area of our lives,it's also egging on all the good girls, all the successful women, and all those who feel defeated to be in charge of our lives as never before. Far more than a whisper but not quite yet a scream, it's saying, "Decide who you want to be and go for it. Look within. Think strategically. Act bodaciously. And love every minute of it!"

Here's An Offer For Bodacious Women Reading This Book!

Dear Bodacious Woman:

Thank you for reading *Bodacious! Career: Outrageous Success for Working Women*. Helping women become and stay bodacious is the focus of my career as an author, speaker, and seminar leader.

As I speak to audiences worldwide, I hear from scores of women who are courageously becoming bodacious. But they aren't doing it alone. Their BoMos (bodacious moments) usually happened with the encouragement of a friend, colleague or loved one. That's why I highly encourage you to get the support you need to thrive in your career!

I have a way to support you as well! Go to my website **bodaciouscareer.com** and subscribe to my eNewsletter, *BODACIOUSLY!* In each edition you'll get:

- Answers to your questions about career challenges

- Practical, up-to-the-minute tips & strategies

- Helpful advice & mentoring

- An opportunity to netconnect with other Bodacious Women

- Free events & invitations

- Special unadvertised discounts & other bodacious goodies

I have a gift to help you get started! When you subscribe to my eNewsletter, you'll immediately receive a copy of my latest mini e-book of fresh ideas for Bodacious Women! It's my "thank-you" for joining me and thousands of women as we bodaciously build our careers and lives together. You'll find your gift, and more, at **bodaciouscareer.com**. **So, don't wait, go there now!**

On your journey, remember the Bodacious Women mantra: *Look Within, Think Strategically, Act Bodaciously, and Love Every Minute of It!* You can do it! I'm here to help.

Here's to our Bodacious Careers and futures!

Cheers,

Mary Foley

Mary Foley

P.S. If you're interested in scheduling me for a seminar or to speak at your company or organization, send an e-mail to mary@bodaciouscareer.com or call my office at 703.251.4899.